S0-CNH-861

GRANDMOTHER EARTH IX: 2003

Photo by Bonnie L. Warner

GRANDMOTHER EARTH
IX: 2003

Patricia Smith
Frances Brinkley Cowden
Editors

Frances Darby
Lorraine Smith
Marcelle Zarshenas
Editorial Assistants

Featuring
Award-winning
Poetry and Prose
from the

2002 GRANDMOTHER EARTH
NATIONAL WRITING CONTEST

And Featuring
FLORIDA WRITERS

GRANDMOTHER EARTH CREATIONS
Memphis, Tennessee

Copyright ©2003 by Grandmother Earth Creations

ALL RIGHTS RESERVED
Individual works belong to the individual authors. This book or parts thereof may not be reproduced without permission from the individual authors or publisher except for customary privileges extended to the press and other reviewing agencies.
Work previously published was used by permission of the individual authors.

Cover Art:
Pencolo Beach, Florida by Barbara Britton Abbott

ISBN 1-884289-22-3 10.00

FIRST EDITION: 2003
GRANDMOTHER EARTH CREATIONS
8432 Wood Shadows Lane
Cordova, TN 38108
Phone: (901) 309-3692
gmoearth@aol.com
www.grandmotherearth.com

We hopefully will stop to consider
All the blessings we've had since birth;
One of the greatest God has provided
Is our home—Grandmother Earth.
--Embree Bolton

Grandmother Earth IX Winners

POETRY: Judge, Clovita Rice

1st   Hand Me My Shadow, N. Colwell Snell, Salt Lake City, UT

2nd   Good-bye Rosemary, Arla M. Clemons, LaCrosse, WI

3rd   What Goes Around, Jeanne Kelly, Madison, MS

4th   Reflections, Malu Graham, Memphis, TN

1HM   Sugar Mountain, Alice Heard Williams, Lynchburg, VA

2HM   April Talking, Leona Mason, Bourbon, MO

3HM   Wild Horses, N. Colwell Snell, Salt Lake City, UT

4HM   Solitude, Frances W. Muir, Coral Springs, FL

HUMOROUS:

1st   Parody on the Night Before Christmas, Auguste R. Black, Huntsville, AL

2nd   Looking Down on Lester's Head, Ruth Whittenberg, Bella Vista, AR

HM   About that Dr. James, Frieda Beasley Dorris, Memphis, TN

ENVIRONMENTAL:

1st   Spending the Butterfly Treasury, Russell H. Strauss

2nd   Life Lines, Jane Allen, Wetumpka, AL

HM   Ghosts of Red Foxes, Elizabeth Howard, Crossville, TN

HM   Solitude, Frances Muir, Coral Springs, FL

HM   Visiting the Nature Preserve, Alice Heard Williams, Lynchburg, VA

SHORT FORM, Judge: Frances Darby
1st   Solitude, Frances W. Muir, Coral Springs, FL
2nd   Poverty, Marcia Camp, Little Rock, AR
HM   Mama's Breakfast, John W. Crawford, Arkadelphia, AR
HM   Buffalo Children, Angela Logsdon, Memphis, TN
HM   Sea of Mind, Adams, Burlington, CA

HAIKU: Judge, Jennifer Jensen
1st   Illumination, Susanne Leeds, Deray Beach, FL
2nd   multicolored trees, Betty Heidelberger, Lexa, AR
1HM   Alzheimer's, Dena R. Gorrell, Edmond, OK
2HM   Escape, Rita Goodgame, Little Rock, AR
3HM   catching, Marilyn Stacy, Dallas, TX
4HM   on a beach, Laurie Boulton, Melbourne, AR
5HM   Mid-spring, Tom McDaniel, Memphis, TN
6HM   grief, Dena R. Gorrell, Edmond, OK
7HM   new snow, Florence Hustedt, Clark Summit, PA

PROSE: Judge, Frank Reed Nichols
1st   Grandpa Knew, Neil Chandler, Mountain Home, AR
2nd   Degrees of Poverty, Miriam Doege, Panama City, FL
3rd   When There's Nothing to Do, Dorothy Hatfield, Beebe,
       AR
1HM: The Day Booger Johnson Died, Neil Chandler, Mountain
       Home, AR
2HM: The Contract, Dorothy Hatfield, Beebe, AR
3HM: Grandma's Roses, Neil Chandler, Mountain Home, AR

HUMOROUS:
1st   Mary Marjorie May, Malra C. Treece, Memphis, TN
HM   Setting up Shop, Faye Hartleben, Amherst Jct., WI

ENVIRONMENTAL
1st   A Bayberry Candle, Cornelius Hogenbirk, Waretown, NJ
HM   Box Turtles and Green Snakes, Christine Henderson,
       Searcy, AR

YOUTH AWARDS
1st   Forever and Never Changing, Melissa Taylor, grade 11,
       Little Rock, AR

2nd	Blast that Guy Shakesphere: He Makes the Rest of us Look Bad, Grade 11, Laurie Skelton, Birmingham, AL
3rd	Wolf, Courtney Watts, Grade 5, Ellicott City, MD
4th	Katie Williams, Domino, Grade 7, Imboden, AR Sometimes, Aishah El-Akkan, Age 14, Daytona Beach, FL
HM	Kite, Christoper Watts, Grade 3, Ellicott City, MD

Eye-poems:

1st	A Night, Sarah Nolen, Grade 12, Memphis, TN
2nd	Drowning, Ticara Gailliard, Grade 12, Memphis, TN
HM	I'm not a Slave, Bethany Byrd, Grade 12, Memphis, TN

FLORIDA AWARDS IN MEMORY OF PETE AND GLADYS BULLARD: Judge, Dorothy Bullard Tacker

POETRY:

1st	haiku, Bonnie Warner, Port Orange, FL
2nd	I Have Worn this Shirt, June Owens, Zephyrhills, FL
HM	Ashes to Ashes, Meg Roman, Zephyrhills, FL
HM	Faded Photographs, Frances W. Muir, Coral Springs, FL

PROSE:

1st	Pressure in Paradise, Audrey Cooke, Daytona Beach, FL
2nd	Rocks: William Caudle, (Florida Native), Summertown, TN

Dragon Mouth Orchis by Neal Hogenberk

IN THE PARKING LOT

I was parking my car by the bookstore
and there you were
leaning on that big black motorcycle,
helmet hung on the gold handlebars.
Traumatized, I sat and watched you.

You were all in black--
shirt, jeans, boots, jacket, all black.
Engrossed in conversation,
you aimed a smile
at that unseen voice on the phone.
Your profile, your hand gestures,
your brownish gray hair
circling your front bald spot,
you were there, totally there ...

I wanted to call to you.
I started to, but knew
all I could do
was to sit there and stare,
absorbing the gift of seeing you again.

That man leaning there in black,
He would have thought I lacked good sense
because you,
my dear fun-loving brother Max,
have been dead three years ...

Clovita Rice

THE BOWL ON THE SHELF

An antique bowl with pedestal legs
graces mother's china cupboard.
Orange concave glass changes tones
when the light shifts. Day after day,
it sits on the shelf looking pretty—
without purpose, never used,
its circle of dust unbroken.

Often, I open the glass door,
run my fingers over the peacock tracings
to feel the arc of the feathered fan.
When I hear mother's footsteps,
I quietly close the door, hoping
she will not hear the squeak of the hinge.

Today that same bowl
is in my dining room hutch.
On special occasions, I place it
on the table where everyone can see it.
It sparkles on a white tablecloth.
I straighten the wrinkles around
the pedestal legs, stand back
to admire the rainbow colors.
At times, I find myself listening
for a sound on the stairs.
I place the bowl back on the shelf
waiting for that familiar voice,
but there is none.

Arla M. Clemons

REFLECTIONS

The stranger at my table
speaks in your voice. The stranger is not young
like you. His eyes, though also kind, are old;
they nearly disappear with every crevassed smile,
and while I must admit

I like the way he talks and what he says,
the more I listen, all the more
my heart asks *where are you?* and how
did this calm personage find out
how I like my tea?

I turn to Honey Bear, bold breakfast table guest
purring in the stranger's lap,
and ask him with my eyes to give some sign, but all
that meets my gaze is amber ice.

The big bay window of the breakfast room
looks out on clouded skies
and summer's greeny gloom, rain-heavy trees,
wet stepping stones dark-bright in sodden grass.

We rise, the two of us, our reflections
mirrored in the mullioned panes
against the darkness of outdoors.
I watch, and see the stranger bend
and kiss the cheek of an old woman.

I read the answer to my question in the glass.

Malu Graham

HAND ME MY SHADOW

Leaves from the cottonwood crackle
under my weight, veins still
cobwebbing tributaries to their outer edges.
So soon from green to this, I count
a few dozen autumns swept away
by pompous gusts like this one
ripping at my face.

Disturbing thoughts rankle
me once more with dull
excuses in lieu of wages
for best laid schemes. What was meant
by that yellow ball of sun swimming free
under the glassy bay, dawn's crimson tone
tagging along behind bright as brass?

It was destroyed by the warp and buckle
of summer's flaming swell,
swept in waves and bulges
by snarling winds, raucous, hell-bent
and winnowing.
I have felt my shadow blown
clean off my back, haunting as a curse.

I shall likely knuckle
under to the relentless coil
of apathy, circling in steady stages
to strangle my discontent.
What began as a tingling mystery
to settle into on a rainy afternoon,
tiptoed piecemeal out of sight like guilty rainbows.

I have gone to clear out my locker,
dufflebag it out the door and down the hall
while that sliver of a moon dodges

the last upward glance my eyes have spent
on grief. Hand me my shadow,
my lone companion,
before the light turns dim and perilous.

N. Colwell Snell

WILD HORSES

There are still places change has not reached
with its nervous fingers, where the sun
has forever hugged the same circles, blotched
scattered buttes and mesas, and scorched
solid rock towers to a deep purple stain--
all sucklings of scarce rains and wind-pocked.

Summer flash floods polish gully walls,
water oozes like lanced blisters,
disappears again into cracks, then crawls
once more inside the earth. Indian paintbrush speckles
the terrain with brilliant bracts, stirs
fiery clusters through the air in wind-whipped intervals.

The blurred horizon holds the swirling dust
of wild horses on the run, their sand-soaked manes
heavy on their necks, tails at half-mast,
vanishing shadows from the past
skimming austere bowels of the plains,
stretching toward the twilight of the West.

N. Colwell Snell

GOOD-BYE ROSEMARY

I wore a wide-brimmed black hat,
trimmed with a velvet ribbon
to Rosemary's funeral.
It would have met her approval.
So stylish at seventy-five,
Rosemary was an addict to purple nail polish
and lavender lace.
It was a cool June—
but the lilacs had made their departure with Rosemary.

The mourners sat on the left of the church.
No one sat on the right.
The pews were blond as sunlight but
hard as butternut. My eyes traveled from
ceiling to pulpit, expecting some sign
of Rosemary's presence.

The choir sang "On Eagle's Wings."
We joined in. I sang the first verse
until a tear rolled down my cheek.
I brushed it away, then turned
to the half-opened stained glass window bringing
in the sunlight and a breeze. A butterfly
made an entrance, fluttered across the church like
a gauzy sail on still water. It landed
in a flower basket, settled between pastel petals.

Through flickering candles
and a cloud of incense, I saw
the butterfly move to a gardenia.
As quivering wings slipped from their cover,
I adjusted my hat, angled it more to the right.
The butterfly soared upward,

exited through the open window following
the beam of the summer sun ...
then it was gone.

Arla M. Clemons

...DUST TO DUST

I do not need to seek revenge
for time will do my work for me
    in the end every enemy
will merely be dusty memory.

La Vonne Schoneman

SILENCE

The house is still and empty, save for us two
we do not speak, it is enough, knowing there is you.
The clock ticks steadily, unafraid a rafter creaks
wind rattles the pane, a sturdy house love has made.
I contemplate a time when you may be away
the silence now is ominous, I want to run and hide.

Walt Stromer

PARODY ON
THE NIGHT BEFORE CHRISTMAS

On the day before Christmas, I sat in my chair.
Still in my gown, no comb through my hair.
The food was all ready to cook and to eat.
The baking was done with many a treat.
But the house! What a mess! The garden was too!
The car was so dirty it didn't look blue,
My attention was called to the skylights above
Being cleaned by a pair of sparkling white gloves.
And leaves in my carport flew up to the sky.
Leaving car and carport clean and dry.
Soon three odd elves came through the door
With vacuums and brooms and mops for the floor,
And dust rags and polish and cleaning supplies.
I couldn't believe what I saw with my eyes.
One put a stool under my feet.
A blanket and pillow made resting complete.
The third brought a cocktail so frosty and red;
Saying, "Relax and rest or we'll put you to bed.
They all started cleaning so thorough and fast
That all I could see was whirlwinds go past.
Ten minutes went by, the cocktail hit home
My eyes and my thoughts did no longer roam.
The twirling and sounds soon put me to sleep
With dreams of delight and slumber complete.
When later I woke, there was no one there.
I smelled turkey and pies and odors so rare.
The house was now spotless, the car was agleam.
The yard was all raked, the puppy was clean.
My hair had been set, my nails had been painted
My dress had been ironed, my shoes recreated.
When out on the porch I heard such a noise,
I knew right away it was my three boys,
With wives and their children and a grandchild or two,
But I was now ready, there was nothing to do.

I hugged and I kissed them and bade them come in
"The food is all ready, let's pray and begin."

Auguste Black

LOOKING DOWN ON LESTER'S HEAD

Lester lives in the house next door.
He's lived there all his life.
He is small and I am tall
but he wants me for his wife.

Lester is an only child
with little authority.
We don't care... though it's not fair ...
it doesn't bother me.

I want to accept his offer,
but I delay instead,
for when he stands next to me,
I look down on the top of his head.

I turned down Eddy Chambers,
as well as his cousin, Fester,
because I really like being with
my next door neighbor, Lester.

My dilemma is tragic.
He's my guy as you can see.
Guess I'll survive until I'm five,
then he may be taller than me.

Ruth Wittenberg

EGRET

A lone white egret
on slim red legs
in shallow shoreline grass

contemplates in silence
the still waters,
looking for food

ADAMS

Photo by Christine Moyer

UNKNOWN WARRIORS

"This is a war of unknown warriors." Winston Churchill

Mr. Churchill, your words
From a decade many of us cannot remember
Have flown to these shores like tired old gulls
Flapping their wings against the winds of change.
Yours was an era when the Luftwaffer
Visited hellfire upon your weary island.
Every night, your fire brigades
Trained hoses on charred London flats
While motors droned and sirens screamed.
Pensioners limping through Piccadilly
To police the blackout, could watch the skies
Turn dawn-red at midnight.
Each day, your housewives queued
Amidst the smoldering rubble
Like dowdy sparrows longing
For nestlings sent for safety to the country.
Yours was an age when canoeists and ferry pilots
Braved restless seas and enemy fire
To rescue an army besieged at Dunkirk.
In speech after speech you told them all
What their hearts already knew,
That they were the warriors behind the lines,
That sanity and freedom would survive.
For sixty years, the world has turned and turned
But the choice remains the same.
We are your unknown warriors, Sir Winston.
Your firemen, your paramedics, your policemen.
Your bankers, farmers, fathers, mothers,
And we shall prevail.
The winds have brought less change than we had hoped.
Your words now rest their feet
In America.

Russell H. Strauss

APRIL TALKING

Just up from the creek,
where the torrent produced
by spring rains has reduced
to sparkling clear water,
which shows its bottom rocks,
And riffles on, in light,
engaging the ear,
as only flowing water can,

along the ridge,
where returning birds
are singing out territory…
there's flint on the path.
The stuff of fire, it was,
for the nations which came
before matches.

The cold spark could wait
through the ages, flint bonded
till strong hands hit chip
against brother chip,
over tinder, projecting
a campfire or a wild burn.

Fire waits through time, for the moment to ignite,
To rise before the wind and vanquish.

Words wait,
till some wordsmith
arranges them together,
an irresistible stress.

Words engage impulse,
invade a million minds,
erupt, and blood flows,
anguish rules,

they call it war.

Could words express harmony
In such terms that everyone
finally GETS IT, all together
and retires mortal conflict
forever?

We are a part of this creation,
as sparks are parts of rocks,
we are born to create, remember this...

Leona Mason Heitsch

A THRUSH CALLS

Death will be only a friend
guiding my footsteps to God
some calm twilight when
hushed winds of night
swing wide the gate
by my garden wall.

Florence M. Hustedt

New snow tops the rim
of the nest in the pear tree
like lemon meringue.

Florence M. Hustedt

THE MOTH

There was a young moth from St. Paul
Who found my mink coat in the hall.
               He ate up one sleeve,
               Not a hair did he leave,
Then took a short nap on the wall.

When he woke he saw that withal
He'd destroyed the coat; ruined it all.
               He felt so inept,
               He wept and he wept.
Did you ever see a moth bawl?

Patricia W. Smith

SEA OF MIND

Ideas, ideas
floating in the sea of mind

get caught, then
wrap themselves in words.

ADAMS

ESCAPE

Slashed red umbrella
slave to piercing wind and rain
flees with broken ribs.

Rita Goodgame

FERRY CROSSING ALONG
THE "TRAIL OF TEARS," 1838

We limped across the ridge at Chattanooga,
Crept serpentine through the Cumberland Plateau,
Tripped down deer trails through the swamps and thickets,
To reach this somber river.
Our feet wrapped in rags,
We are herded aboard the ferry,
Soon the spirits of the oak and elm
Will bid us farewell forever.
We are bound for the land of whispering grass
And empty sky.

For centuries, we Cherokee
Thrived in the womb of our mother forest.
When the white man taught us to wear breeches
And Sequoia taught us to read,
They called us a civilized tribe.
Now we sob for infants starving at the breast,
For elders writhing in the ditches,
For cousins choking with the cholera.
Once assured of sovereignty and peace,
We are dandelion puffs in the winds of change.
Once settled and free,
We are marching for eight hundred miles.

The eastern bank recedes. The cottonwoods
Are sentinels that guard the marsh.
We shall weep a river wider than this Mississippi
And deeper than the lake of heaven,
A river so vast that we could not ferry its waters
In twenty thousand lifetimes.
We shall weep forever.

Russell H. Strauss

YOU CAN'T CAPTURE A RAINBOW

The day the crabs ate my pompano
it taught me
you can't capture a rainbow,
take it out of the sky
and still expect it to glow.

Bettye Kramer Cannizzo

UNDER A SALMON PINK SKY

Where the loon rests in
her bower of lichens and poppies,
amid the glories of Earth's womb
narwhales glide majestically
in the glacial blue-green sea
as if guarding the nursery.

Bettye Kramer Cannizzo

POVERTY

wears the face of a child, big-eyed with hunger, who,
hearing for the first time of tooth-fairy magic,
tears six teeth from her small mouth, rocking
molars till they become ample exchange
for the pillow's trove of coins
that will never come.

Marcia Camp

BUFFALO CHILDREN

With your sun-drenched skin,
brown like the earth that gave you life
your dark eyes pierce my soul
questioning why the buffalo have gone

Angela Logsdon

BEFORE THE FACTORY CLOSED

High class cologne preceded him as he walked
into the concrete room of loud talking women.
He wore a funeral suit like it
was made for him, and varnished black shoes.

Talk stopped. Machines whirred. Nimble fingers
fed fabric to the needle of their machines ever faster,
as he strode front to back and
side to side writing notes on a legal pad.

At noon the women rushed outside
to light up Pall Malls and Virginia Slims.
The gray sky was heavy
as they huddled outside the factory door.

Rain drops pelted the black Mercedes
parked in the owner's space.

Nina Salley Hepburn

YESTERDAY, THESE TREES

Yesterday, the maple and oak
excited in autumn sunlight.
This morning their leaves, hurried
by last evening's wind, returned
without complaining to the earth.
My neighbor stands where
good neighbors not needing
good fences stand. He asks
if he may do my raking.
He gathers color from this—
his giving and taking. He'll press leaves
between wax paper and mail them
to his seven-year-old granddaughter
in Florida. He tells me, "I want
to prepare her for all seasons."

Ellen Hyatt

THE COLOR IN THE SKY

The orange of the sunset
blazes across the sky;
how different if everything were this color.

A minute ago the world had no color,
it might as well as have been grey.

The cat does not care about any of this,
he pays no heed to the orange streak in his fur,
or the grey on his face.

Brett Taylor

GHOSTS OF RED FOXES

Blood calls to blood,
spirit to spirit,
eye to eye.
As though answer
to a vision quest,
a red fox stands long
in my childhood path.
Awe seizes me--
her majesty and grace,
head high,
nose taking my measure,
tail sweeping the air.
We walk away,
looking back,
comrades traveling
this path together,
me unwitting member
of the Fox Clan,
red hair the sign.

The memory as dim
as blanched blood stains,
I go my way,
no backward look,
until I hear of another fox—
disemboweled,
tail cut off,
tooth gouged out,
savaged body thrown
into a ditch,
rain rushing all night,
the creek sucking up
blood and corruption.

Were I bearer
of tail and tooth,

profane trophies,
I would bury them
in the fencerow,
erect a shrine,
beseech forgiveness,
lest fox ghosts
beset my path,
eyes glittering,
tails sweeping,
my blood frozen
in the marrow.

Elizabeth Howard

Photo by Christine Moyer

WHERE THE WILD IRIS GROW

Today I take the upper path to the pond
past the apple tree.
Determined branches whorl outward,
gravid with unborn fruit,
and petals the scattered pink
of predawn sky.
In limitless night beneath the tree
braided roots: apple, shadbush,
fennel and wild plum, rapacious
hedgerow guests
burrow and funnel out of their birth-bed
the precious milk of sun and rain.

This day I am searching
for wild iris and solitude
along the margin of the woods
in dappled folds of ash
near fallow fields
burned of broom sage and clover,
of rabbits' nests and crickets;
and in happier summers a goldfinch
hunting ground.

I see them!
Tiny audacious violet fire
reaching into death
and finding life:
a silent witness to my searching
so strong it could be the chalice
delivering the salve
of earth-borne solitude.

Ruth L. Stewart

VIRGIN LAND

Through the deep hush
of darkness,
I follow a lantern-light
dancing in front
like a will-o'-the-wisp
and thread my way between
vine-covered trees,
over leaf-felted paths,
no more than tracks,
where the light feet of foxes
and white-bellied possums
have trodden in darkness
in a ghost-like tread.

Within the muteness
of that woodland world,
only the moon-tipped trees
had the temerity to speak
and their voices were
but a sweet shiny whisper
that trembled into a quiet sigh.

In the dreamful rest of night,
the startled owl, who hears the
pine needles crackle under my feet,
asks the melancholy question…
"who? who?"

Anne-Marie Legan

SPENDING THE BUTTERFLY TREASURY

This bursary of butterflies
is an Arctic fir forest that has survived
since the ice age on tropic mountaintops.
Here millions of monarchs
rest midway in their migrations.
As we fly overhead,
butterfly clusters become pennies
tossed on a green velvet counter.
Monarchs eat nothing here, but rest their wings
before flitting northward to become
bangles in summer gardens.

Here in Michoscan, the Masagua Indians,
have nothing but logs to sell.
Timber buys frijoles negroes
or tortilla flour to fill
the bloated bellies of their children
Peons with few pesos,
the Masagua spend butterflies.

Monarchs leave the dusty, thinning forests
to drink in nearby lowlands,
wasting precious strength,
Some journey too early into frost,
A fragile treasure is being spent
to feed the destitute of Mexico.

Russell H. Strauss

FLUSHING CEMETERY'S MONUMENT TO SEPTEMBER 11, 2001

A soft sun
Glistens

An ebony marble monument
Mirrors trees

Sitting
In a Peace Garden
Birds sing
And
I lament our loss
Amid the scent of leaves

And
A subtle bird
Peeps out of a knothole.

Vincent J. Tomeo

Also published in *The Edgz*, September, 2002, Vol. 4.

MYSTICAL

Love joins hands and hearts
encircling friends and foes
views the sweet, the bittersweet
tugs gently as it flows
through storms and strife.
It calmly radiates
warms and glows.

Frances Darby

THUNDER IN THE NIGHT

Awakened by the crash of thunder in the night,
I'm reminded of Memphis in June,
And sultry summers at their height,
With Southern storms outwitting a Southern moon.
I'm taken there with lightning brightening up the skies
And thunder tearing through the air.
Colorado's charm is in the way snow flies.
So Spring rains always take me back "there."
If I lose a bit of sleep
It really, really is all right.
If my dreams all lie in a jumbled heap,
I still love the sound of thunder in the night.

Betty Gifford

WHAT GOES AROUND ...

Spinning back through time's tunnel
I sit, a senior in English class
on a bright March afternoon
writing sassy notes to male dolts
caged in desks surrounding me.
My missives flood lined paper, spelling furtive hints
of author worried about date to prom.

Like a mighty empress at the big desk.
a frazzled teacher fights to prize open closed minds.
From her acerbic tongue barbed insults fly,
sticking like thumbtacks to the cluttered cork board of our
minds.
Occasional prints of unsought knowledge
splinter past social urgencies.

as Madeline's "Eve of St. Agnes" adventure
beckons my reverie.

Spinning forward through time's maze,
I stand before a class of senior English students,
a frazzled teacher fighting
to force feed minds convinced that their social verities
supersede truths observed by Keats.
Their youth limits discernment
of "forever young" concepts on Grecian urns.
My acerbic tongue sends rebukes like thumbtacks
nailing the cork board of their closed minds.
Perhaps something permanent occasionally
sticks in tiny apertures
thrust open by persistent snips.

Pricked by a sharp barb from my tutoring,
one of those youths,
now preoccupied with fears
of imminent social disasters,
may even seek to share universal truths
with a future generation.

Jeanne S. Kelly

Photo by Brett Taylor

FRANKLIN D. ROOSEVELT, 73, SUCCUMBS

Four times he was elected President;
four times he earned the people's confidence.
The great depression reeled this continent
so FDR signed laws that made good sense.
The "New Deal" he developed for Relief---
Recovery---Reform---stuck like barbed wire,
restored man's faith and genuine belief
that he could earn at jobs he could acquire.
New programs---WPA and CCC
were household names supplying daily bread;
and Social Security came to be
the answer to our hopes for days ahead.
His Fireside Chats calmed folks. In WWII
we learned exactly what he planned to do.

My Grandma idolized this "Poor Man's King"
and framed his photo in The Litchfield Herald
for her piano. You should have heard her sing
approval for his deeds. Grandma upheld
those ration books he issued during war,
detached, with pride, each stamp for sugar, meat
and shoes; joined paper drives for FDR;
prayed earnest Baptist Prayers we'd soon defeat
our enemies. She sold a dozen eggs
to join The March of Dimes since Polio
had stricken FDR and maimed his legs.
He could not yield to pain with dreams to sow.
I can't forget the way my Grandma cried
the day the radio announced he died.

Verna Lee Hinegardner

GARDENING

she cut back and uprooted, pulled out things that
would not grow yet
took up space

she emptied containers, lopped off spent blooms to
allow new growth
where growth is

she breathes
even as do her flowers

constantly tending, she tends to over tend
fuss too much
perhaps get in the way of the natural order of things

of seeds already planted
primed to open and
be all they are programmed to be

the mighty oak, the full flower, the fruits of passion
all already are

WE already are
programmed for growth, personal and spiritual

All – there's the rub... AND...
not one or the other–but Both
find Self within Self
even as the flower is within the seed

Elaine R. Howard

Old Wooden Water Tower, Tallassee, AL, by Jane Allen

LIFE LINES

The ancient shadow stretched
toward the toasting sun,
wounded by time—beaten by weather.
The naked vitals choked
from light's deft fingers
doomed by life—destined by ill winds.
The wobbly legs splintered
from encrusting mud,
cracked by age—worn by nature's wrath.
The withered beard snarled
around the leaning limbs,
twisted by fate—splattered by raindrops.
A falling wooden tower, now a relic,
weeps for the gushing sound
Of the liquid that once breathed life and
soul into a small southern town.

Jane E. Allen

Bold red lady bug
Dotted upon a soft fern
Wonder to behold!

Diana Kwiatkowski Rubin

**Bettye Cannizzio and her husband, Walter on their
honeymoon in 1946**

SUGAR MOUNTAIN

I want to walk your paths
until I am old and panting at every step,
breathe in the sharpness of your air
beneath lacy branches of the balsam trees
swaying like fan dancers.

I want to surprise foraging wrens
in the thickets,
hurry along your slopes with grandchildren
looking for pink clusters of laurel
and coral petals of wild azalea
growing near fern-filled dells.

I want to see coin dots of moss speckling trunks
of your trees like the backs of old ladies' hands,
hear arias of the tiny warblers
high overhead,
spot their sulfur feathers among the leaves
if I'm lucky.
I want to see a wild turkey family cross the path,
babies capped like princelings
in fuzzy down,
show Robert and Peter the mottled Emperor moth,
napping on a rhododendron blossom.
But how long will it all last?

Every hour traffic swells,
snarled like balls of knitting
in the valley below.

Construction sounds march closer,
impinging on my solitude.
The timber mill belches smoke, pollutes the stream.
How long can you hold out, Sugar Mountain?

Alice Heard Williams

ELEPHANT BONES

I drive to my farmhouse in the country
where late the bluebird sings of "bare mined choirs,"
a splintered head board takes root among the weeds.
Half lunacy, to glean through the curled photos,
the smell of our dog still anchored in the air. A box
of expired heart-worm pills lie impotent above the sink.
The derelict change I gather from the carpeted ruts
shines no brighter at my urging.
Not that, in Spring, the kitchen floor would chafe
under my scouring stroke; the warming light
to each, holds up our own truancy
of last year's Burpee seed planning calendar.
Tacked to the wall beside the kitchen window
a red X on May 10 marks the frost-free date,
envoy from some past ripeness.

Meanwhile, 1, with the remote control
am channel surfing on a Friday evening
when I should be baking pizza for our ghost child
or feigning youth at the taco bar slash
happy hour at TGI Fridays,
licking the hot sauce from my fingers
while I explain my profession to
a guy undressing me inside the booth of his head.
Now I've flipped to a PBS documentary
about elephants in an eastern Kenya reserve;
how the herd mourns the passing of their leader
by running slender trunks over the mound of bones.
Snorting out dust, a lone male caresses each fragment
like a relentless suitor of his lost love.

Theresa Brown

MOCKINGBIRD

In his neat gray suit,
whiteshirted like
a businessman,
musician and mimic,
he dazzles with his
impromptus.

Therese Arceneaux

THE WIND OF MANY PLACES

I listen to the wind,
for it speaks in many tongues
and tells of many places
now and past. It blows
in warm, Sisyphean gusts
across the mystic desert sands,
sneaking through the open tents
of some drifting Scheherazade
who spins tales of ancient love.
It is an errant, prairie storm,
wild and dangerously beautiful,
lost on a sea of billowing grass,
rising gracefully yet quickly dying
without one knowing of its beauty.
It is the raw, untamed anger
of a biting, December blizzard,
swirling ghostly dervish-like
and sifting delicate, gossamer snow
into every crevice of the frozen earth.
They speak to me,

these winds of many places,
and I listen to their myriad voice,
for it is the pulse of the land,
the heartbeat of all the lost souls.

Yet, somewhere, I am told,
there is a soft and gentle wind
that rises with some rickety moon
into a virgin night of first love;
and then life is, for an instant, sweet,
like honeysuckle breath, and each moment
is a window that opens into all time.
So take me with you, wind of many places,
and scatter me, like autumn leaves,
along the paths that lead back to
some hidden place beyond reality.

James B. Copening

DES MAGIES ECOSAISES

Purple heather waves;
Mist and moor stretch beyond view;
wind haunted Highlands.

Thomas W. McDaniel

Mid spring gathering:
Sprigs, threads, twigs, egg cache garland,
Mockingbird twitters.

Thomas W. McDaniel

CICADA SPRING

As sun warms earth in seventeenth spring
You swell
Shudder
Stretch
Scratch
And emerge into spring

In sun warmed earth for sixteen springs
Your insect body grew
Bulging copper eyes,
Copper veined transparent wings,
Fragile folding legs,
And voice to sing in seventeenth spring.

At sunrise in seventeenth spring
A thousand Cicada mating calls
Softly mewling
Gently rising
Crescendo at midday to deafening din
And slowly fall again
To sundown silence.

By summer's dawn your song is gone.
Mute carcasses cling to trees
And strew wooded paths where predators feed.
Your cycle is complete
Till next seventeenth spring
When you will wake again. And sing!

Martha McNatt

LOVELY PASSING

The woods are breathing quietly today:
Cicadas drone, birds walk demurely here,
And butterflies are testing yet the way
Of destiny in lazy circles, fear
Of change delayed for now in making last
This moment. Leaves release their green in stillness-
Taking instead first hints of summer past,
Tinges of subtle colors, without sadness.
The strewn, an ancient mirror, reflects tall
Leaning weeds, primly nodding flowers, and
Cattails holding themselves aloof though fall
Comes. Such stiff defiance the rippled sand,
Their shallow home, can honor for awhile;
Then they will loose their tightness with a smile.

Winifred Hamrick Farrar

Alzheimer's grips my
Mother ... I hold her empty
shell and feel homesick.

Dena R. Gorrell

Grief sits, large as an
elephant, upon the heart
when a loved one dies.

Dena R. Gorrell

AN INCISED CRESCENT

Beneath a dead cottonwood,
its branches,
claws against the wind, rises
the sweet curve of a coyote's throat,
crying to the moon,
that moon shrunk to a fine
crescent incised on sky.

Remember day's
lenticular clouds, sleek
as wings of migrating geese
in sunsweet air,
remember the freedom of sand,
wild grasses.

Subtle as the memory of smell,
the poems hang
in the air like leaves.

Rosalyn Ostler

Multicolored trees
Form a perfect frame for fall
Winter will not wait.

Betty Heidelberger

POEM

the curving path
of morning's light
filters through blue-eyed windows
sending shadows scurrying

like mice pursued
then invitingly beckons
to lift my mind's foggy veil
revealing a bride's radiance
one quiet virgin moment
affirming a bridegroom's patience
with me the lone attendant
the witness of this holy rite
the marriage of paper and pen
consciousness consummated
indwelling - compelling
be fruitful - multiply
in soul's embrace
my image trace
'til death do us part
the flesh made word

Rebecca Davis Henderson

all these tourists
too busy to notice
the yellow butterfly

Kolette Montague

LAUGHTER OF DEAD WOMEN

I hear the laughter
of dead women
in a room full of
sighs and shadows
 rose water
and lilies

I gaze into that
narrow room
as into a tomb
or a painting
dark with smoke
from lamps
long broken
and swept away

With pale hands
they beckon me
to listen and
understand
moving slowly
they talk in
whispers
I can't quite make out

jet beads gleam
on black silk bosoms
their hair piled
high, swept up
with silver combs
laughing they
feed a solemn child
sips of blackberry wine
and slivers of
almond cake

and haunt me
with stories
I can't quite make out

Nancy R. Hamner

HOLIDAY FEVER

I worked with a lady once,
an old maid who lived alone
and had outlived her people.

Early July, late December,
she'd throw a fit right there on the job.
Co-workers whispered, "Holiday fever?"

In time, we pieced it together:
Reunions, families, fried chicken.
"Don't start, you hear me!

"I don't want to know about
your picnics and potato salad."
Time and again she yelled, "Spare me!"

Now I've been alone a while,
I get it... too late to comfort her.
Sometimes I come down with holiday fever.

Florence Bruce

From: *THE OZARK MOUNTAINEER*, **December, 2001**

VISITING THE NATURE PRESERVE

On the edge of the water
the raccoon in full, ring-tailed glory
raises his paw from the muddy shallows
where he's washing a breakfast morsel.
Shiny, black marble eyes, unblinking,
regard us, not afraid but alert.
Moving along the boardwalk
we hear a scrub jay calling the alarm.
A clutch of sand crabs
scurry below us, vanishing
into tiny holes, home,
in the coarse, dark sand.

The mangrove throbs, teems, pulsates
with life, in and out of the brackish water,
a lush habitat for bird, animal, insect.
Decay carpets the forest floor,
plants live and die, returning
to the soil and water in regular, repeating cycle.
Trees and shrubs shelter inhabitants
from the merciless sun beating down.

Suddenly we come upon an alligator below,
stretched full length
on a decaying log at swamp's edge,
basking in a patch of sunlight.
Two tiny, perfect copies drape themselves
over their mother's back.
Where mangroves meet
the intercostal waterway, blue herons
and white ibis stand, long ballerina legs
and graceful necks alert for food
among the reeds. Pelicans in precise
formation swoop overhead as though
on parade. And although we cannot see them,

we know there are manatees
below the surface, waiting for quiet to emerge.

Alice Heard Williams

^^

catching fresh breezes
eagles glide on unmarked paths
celebrating life
Marilyn Stacy

A VETERAN'S CEMETERY

Up from a grave's tan gray bed
Pop little white heads
Mushrooms dance to a pine wind

Leaves are dust
Quarrel with the sun

Pleached golden trees
Splash upon a rust earth

Casting shadows
Of angel's wings

Bagpipers play taps
Against a red moon.

Vincent J. Tomeo

WINDY AFTERNOON

Rivers of wind
rush through the treetops
all afternoon,
birds ride the crests
of leaf-surf.

Therese Arceneaux

PAYING THE PRICE

As I travel from Bakersfield
on Highway 5, I spy
hundreds of windmills
east of Oakland
at Altamont Pass.
They cavort
upon hill after hill
with synchronized whirl,
like cloned acrobats,
metal arms turning
rapidly, rhythmically
in afternoon sun.

In sharp contrast,
green-shod and demure,
those California hills huddle
like beaten children,
their pride pricked
by such callous display
of three-armed titans
poking from myriad ridges
into blue envelope of sky.

Principles of wind power

amaze me.
I first saw them at work
in experimental fields
on a long stretch of lava beds
in Hawaii. At that time
I thought *how great.*
But now I keep wondering
what is the price - the overlapping
price of power?

Bonnie S. Gudmundson

MAMA'S BREAKFAST

The mellow aroma of Folger's
glides through the kitchen air
merging with the pungent smell of crisp, cured ham
cooking in the cast-iron skillet—
memories of Mama's morning ritual.

John W. Crawford

PENGUIN STYLE

Stand tall
young waiter, dark --
wearing long your tuxedo
in shining white with black flaps in
the wind.

John W. Crawford

ABOUT THAT DR. JAMES
(On extracting a stubborn tooth)

Now dear Dr. James stuck his thumb in my mouth
And suddenly all of my senses went south.

He prized and he prodded and sawed on my tooth
And the pain was like thunder—I tell you the truth.

I hollered and prayed and tore at my hair
Convinced I would croak in this mad dentist's chair.

He'd grab the needle and stab me once more
And I was like puddles of blood on the floor.

"Bite down," he would say - "Now bite, bite, bite, bite—"
Then had the raw nerve to ask, "Are you all right?"

He twisted and hammered—then plumb out of breath
Swore he'd get that sucker or poke me to death.

When all else had failed, he resorted to force.
He reared back like Samson and plotted his course.

Rammed his foot on my chest and with one mighty clout
He fell over backward and yanked that dude out.

Then I was like jelly—a pure basket case
With legs gone all wobbly and blood on my face.

But I must confess that after such grief
I had the sensation of perfect relief.

And when I have tooth pain, I call Dr. Jim—
But sometimes I fancy a toothache for him.

Frieda Beasley Dorris

WHERE HE HAD BEEN

Flying on the swings my father made
two planks on chains that hung from the
huge log placed between the tall cottonwood trees
I dreamed of worlds I would conquer
with my intellect and imagination,
I thought be my inheritance.
The fuzz of the cottonwood seeds
floated all around like descending helicopters
mingling with the dust of the cars on the gravel road
which I breathed as a rite of passage
into the outside world.
The rhythm of the swings rocked me into fantasy.
as the whispering leaves witnessed my
impending fame

With bare feet I followed the furrows of Daddy's plow
watching to avoid earthworms
marveling at the softness of the fresh-turned earth
forgetting how hard the sun-baked ground would be
in a few weeks when we hoed the cotton
row by row—
slave to the weeds and the maddening sun.

And on the same road where he drove
the big Ford truck to the cotton gin
and brought back school clothes, oranges and apples,
we walked past the cotton fields to a country school
where ribbons of knowledge intoxicated us.

The day before his funeral I sat
in his the brown leather-like recliner
where he dozed for hours each day when he became
too tired to make swings, to plow fields
or to haul cotton.
As people brought in food in a steady stream

I sat the whole day not even getting up to eat.

But it did not bring him back—not even for a moment.

Frances Brinkley Cowden

HOW MANY SNOWFLAKES DOES IT TAKE TO FILL A RIVER

No question about what belongs
to a river, like first snowflakes
diving from Thanksgiving skies
to become one with old
river water whose sides
slap virgin silt at land's edge,

Countless patterned flakes,
barely seen in their swift fallen fame,
engulfed in a plight to ride the
river south into warm Gulf waters,
past solemn farms of winter,
toward the ocean where snowfall
is but a Northern dream. Flakes
dissolve in river water and like
beautiful moments go unheard,
brief as breath exhaled in the cold,
to become one with a body of water
that has a lifetime collection of perfect
holiday snowflakes, the number it takes
to fill a river.

Judith Bader Jones

Sun's rays creep across
the room whirl around on a
trip through yesterdays

Laura Pheonix

**Curtis Davis c1915, Cullman, Alabama, father
of Rebecca Davis Henderson**

GRANDPA KNEW

Neil Chandler

Just past mid-afternoon, thick dark clouds climbed high above the western horizon. Grandpa recognized the weather change perhaps twenty minutes before the first thunder echoed across the hills of Lincoln County, Missouri. He called to me, then unhitched the horses as I slid to the ground. Without a word he slapped reins against their flanks and walked them toward the barn. I followed behind, double-stepping to keep up. Now, the horses stood quietly in a passageway between the stalls, welcoming an interruption of their work pulling a cultivator amid rows of young corn stalks. And on this day, they shared the added burden of a small boy on their backs. To them maybe a chore, but to me a ride on horseback highlighted a 1940 summer vacation at my grandparents' farm.

Grandpa Abb Watson farmed with horses, raised seven children, radiated physical strength, spoke sparingly, and faithfully each Sunday sang a booming bass in nearby Harmony Grove Church. His presence often intimidated me...even into his eighth decade of existence ... but throughout my experience with him, he drew me and my increasing inquisitiveness near like iron filings to a magnet. Until I reached busy teenage years, I enjoyed the warmth of many summer vacation weeks exploring his farm ... and learning about life.

As the storm neared, I jerked with each flash of wild electricity and burst of thundering drum roll, but Mollie and Babe took little notice. This working pair had witnessed many thunderstorms and only flicked their tails, scattering hordes of hungry flies gathered in the barn.

I crowded close to Grandpa's side, while two stories high above rain rattled against the corrugated metal roof. I sought security and some assurance I might survive the lightning bolts that flared with greater intensity as the storm released energy absorbed from the hot July day. Grandpa did not tease or laugh-he surely saw my fright-but calmly turned and selected a halter hanging from a peg on the wall of the harness area where we waited. He pulled on the straps, testing the strength of the stitches, then handed the halter to me.

"Smell it." he said. "Rain always brings out the oil."

I took the halter and lifted the straps to my nose. "It smells good," I said, momentarily forgetting the violent storm slashing outside.

"Sure does," he agreed. "I suppose I've smelled well-oiled leather thousands of times, but it takes a moment like this when Mother Nature stops our work for a man to appreciate the things he handles every day."

"I've smelled this somewhere else, Grandpa, but I don't remember where." I pressed the halter again to my nose. "Smells like cinnamon."

He clasped his hands around his right knee and, lifting the leg slightly, leaned back on the bench until he rested against rough-sawn boards that kept the rain at bay. "I suspect you have, boy, and if you're lucky you'll know the smell many times again. It's the smell of working animals. Leather from a cow long gone to heaven…if there is such a place…and the sweat from ol' Mollie and Babe mixed with harness oil to keep the straps from getting brittle."

The noise from the downpour slackened and I squirmed, wanting to get up and look outside. I had sat too long in one place. I handed Grandpa the black halter and started toward the door, but he stopped me.

"Only a short respite," he said. "The next wave will come along in a matter of minutes."

"How do you know, Grandpa?" I asked. "Looks like it's getting lighter out there. It's just sprinkling now."

"Better wait," he said gently. "Your grandma will likely skin you alive if you traipse through the mud and track it into the house."

Those words stopped me. I didn't want to get on the wrong side of the cook, for she'd planned fried chicken and cornbread for the supper table. I turned away from the door ... and jumped with fright when a brilliant flash from the promised second assault barely faded before an earsplitting crash of thunder pounded our shelter.

"That one was pretty close." Grandpa nodded and made a clucking sound through his teeth. "Do you know the way to tell how close a lightning bolt has struck?"

"By how loud the thunder sounds," I guessed.

"Well, that might give you an idea, but if you'll start counting slowly when you see lightning and continue until you hear thunder, you can figure it out."

"How, Grandpa?" I asked. "How can that tell how far away lightning hit?"

"Do you know how far a mile is?"

I thought an instant before I answered. "I know Dad said it's forty long and mighty hard miles from here to our house in town."

His eyes sparkled and what may have been a chuckle escaped from his chest. "The schoolhouse up the road is about a mile from here. If I were to go up there and make a loud noise...say maybe fire my shotgun...how long do you think it would take before you heard it if you waited here in the barn?"

"That old gun's so loud, I guess I'd hear it right when you pulled the trigger," I said. Then I frowned. "Wouldn't I?"

"Would you believe you could count to five from the time you saw the puff of smoke from the barrel until you heard the noise?" He glanced at the disbelief in my expression then continued. "I don't remember who worked it out, but sound travels about a thousand feet a second. And since there's a little more than 5,000 feet in a mile, it takes about five seconds to travel that far. You don't realize it because most things you hear are close to you."

I paused a few seconds. "Like when thunder just now came right when the lightning flashed...and sometimes they're far apart."

"You figured it out." This time a grin blossomed. "The last strike hit right close. Let's count the next time we see the lightning."

Now I waited near the barn door, anxious for the clamor that accompanied this storm. When the flare came, I began to count out loud.

"Slow," Grandpa said and helped with the cadence.

"One thousand three, one thousand four, one thousand five," we said, finishing together as a loud clap interrupted our count.

"That one's a mile away!" I shouted. "It can't hurt me when it's so far away!" I looked out the door at the retreating storm.

"You're right," he agreed. "But watch out for this one!" And he slammed the halter across two empty, metal feed buckets causing a tremendous clatter.

"Grandpa!" I shouted, trying hard to swallow and push down a huge lump in my throat. "You scared me to death!"

"Yeah, but I suspect you'll never be frightened by a lightning storm again." He laughed, stood and pulled me close. "Guess we'd better take the harness off Mollie and Babe. It'll be too wet to go back to the corn field today."

Whistling softly, he started toward the waiting animals. "But first, put this back where it belongs." He handed me the halter.

I stood on tiptoe to reach the peg on the barn wall. As I slipped the smooth leather into its proper place, I smelled once more its aroma. I've often wondered if Grandpa watched while I held the straps close to my nose or, with his lesson complete, did he simply move on to the next chore without looking back? Regardless, when a first roll of distant thunder reaches my ears today, I recall with warmth a treasured time when a man and a barn provided needed comfort and shelter. Then I watch for a flash and begin to count.

MARY MARJORIE MAY

Malra Treece

Nobody ever calls her just plain Mary, because that she is not. She used to live next door before she moved to Montreal nine years ago.

Almost every morning she came over for coffee so that we could talk. Then after she went home I telephoned her. George, my husband, thinks I spend too much time on the telephone; I still call Mary Marjorie May once or twice a week, or she calls me. George doesn't remember that she moved to Montreal, although I have told him a dozen times. He never listens, especially at breakfast. It's true the telephone bills are rather high—well, really high—but I always tell George the exact amount at breakfast, knowing that he isn't listening anyway.

A few weeks ago our conversation was different from usual. "Mary Marjorie, is that really you? In London? Your bossy old answering machine gave a number and it was the Ritz Hotel in London! My goodness, how do you feel?"

"Oh, I feel awful," she said, "I have laryngitis, bronchitis, tendonitis, colitis, probably appendicitis—"

"Mary Marjorie, don't you have anything wrong with you that doesn't rhyme?" I asked. "But I didn't mean your ailments. I mean how happy you must be to be on vacation in London—I'd like to go to London."

"What did you say, Mary Marjorie? Did I hear you correctly? There must be something wrong with this phone. Did you say that you are in London with your boy friend? I don't care whether you have separate rooms or not—oh, you do have separate rooms? That's not what I'm interested in right now—and I don't believe you, anyway. You probably went on some kind of senior-citizens tour. Well, anyway, you'd better change your terminology. I'm sure in this case—even if you're halfway telling the truth, the word 'boy' doesn't fit."

"You're kidding me, aren't you? A 28-year old hunk? Where did you ever learn that word? Where would you ever find a 28-year-old, hunk or not, or anybody else—no, no, Mary Marjorie, I didn't mean that the way it sounded. Mary Marjorie, please don't hang up—I just thought, well, you know—it's not that you are unattractive—I just meant that I thought you had more sense—no—please don't hang up. What I meant to say was I thought you didn't have enough money, I know you must be paying all the bills—no, it's none of my business—but there's this moral question, too—I guess that is an old-fashioned word, yes, I know it is the year two thousand and two—"

"Mary Marjorie, don't you breathe a word of this to my George," I told her. "You know how old-fashioned he is. Yes, I realize you are not likely to see him, but he thinks you still live next door. He might ask you to move. What's that? Did you ask me if my dear husband is stupid? You know he's not stupid—he's just well—I can't exactly find the word for it right now—anyway, if he's not a completely perfect husband, at least I have one, no, don't be angry, I didn't mean to insult you. I'll bet you could find a husband even at your age if you really wanted one—but don't marry the hunk, he just wants your money, in case you have any—"

She hung up on me.

I called Mary Marjorie again, this time to apologize. She laughed. "What's that?" I asked. "You were just kidding——you were playing a trick on me? Well, I knew all along you were kidding. I wouldn't believe a story like that. What's that? A writer who happens to be in the same hotel? He's helping you write your autobiography? Now, Mary Marjorie May, I know absolutely for sure and for certain that you are still kidding me, stop it, please, you have never done anything worth writing a whole book about, why would even a starving writer help you write your autobiography? No, no, I didn't mean it that way—don't hang up again, please don't hang up."

"She hung up on me again," I said to George, who had come down for breakfast.

"Who hung up on you?"

"Mary Marjorie May!"

"Who is she? Oh, now I remember. She's the skinny gal next door."

"George, Mary Marjorie doesn't live next door any more. She moved to Montreal nine years ago."

"Is that so? I didn't see a moving van."

"She sneaked away in the dead of night."

"But she must live next door. You were just talking to her."

"There's a new-fangled service they call long distance."

"You mean you were calling her in Montreal? In Montreal, Canada?"

"No, not to Montreal."

"Good, it must cost a lot of money to telephone someone in Canada."

"The call was to London."

"Oh, then that's OK. Who is in London?"

"Mary Marjorie May."

"The skinny gal who lives next door?" he asked. "I noticed I haven't seen her lately."

"George, I want to ask you something," I said, "is it all right with you if I find a young hunk and go on a vacation in London?"

"Let's go," he said.

So that's why we went to London. We left right away before George changed his mind.

A BAYBERRY CANDLE

Cornelius Hogenbirk

"A bayberry candle burned to the socket brings luck to the house and gold to the pocket."

If there was a snippet of truth in the above whimsical quip, it sure would justify the purchase of a few bayberry candles to give 'em a try. The truth is that this is one of the many such folklore quips that are only fairy tales. Quips that one recounts with tongue in cheek.

However I do have a liking for the clean, somewhat spicy scent that a burning bayberry candle gives forth. For that reason and the reason that follows, I will touch flame to a bayberry candlewick.

During the winter holiday season, the days are at their shortest, and the sun has seemingly gone off on an extended vacation. It is dark when I get up, and hours before my bedtime it becomes dark once again. All that is needed is a stretch of wearisome winter weather to send my spirits down into the dumps.

It is at a time such as this that I will light my bayberry candles, in order to chase Dr. Gloom out of my house. A pair of them are on the stone mantelpiece on top of my fireplace. A shaded 7 ½ watt night light is the only other light in the room. The fireplace is prepped for its gloom-away role, but for the moment left asleep.

The candlelight sometimes wavers, in pretty little dance steps. At other times it flutters from wafts of mysterious origin and chases the scent to where I sit. In short order I am pleasantly sedated. Ongoing candlelit daydreaming now mellows my formerly wintry mood, and I am no longer down in the dumps.

The time has come, in this essay, to flicker on from candlelight seduction, to bayberry bush enlightenment. The bayberry bush, sometimes called, the wax-myrtle, *Myrica pennsylvanica*, is still plentiful, here along the Jersey shore line, in areas that are still open to Mother Nature's nurture. It is a rather homely, semi-evergreen plant, deciduous—separate male and female plants.

In April to May yellowish catkins appear. They too are rather homely, having neither sepals or petals. The love of a sea breeze takes care of the pollination. During the growing season, clusters of hard, round drupes mature along the plant's woody stems. The small "berries" are coated with a grayish-white wax. Though they are inedible to us, certain of the birdies have an appetite for them, including the myrtle warbler, bluebird, chickadee and robin.

Early-day settlers discovered that the bayberry plant had medicinal values. A bayberry tea tonic was said to cure a sore throat and jaundice and ease nasal congestion and "spongy gums." A root bark poultice was used to help heal ulcers, cuts and bruises. Ladies who detected a wrinkle or two in their tinplate mirror reflections used a bayberry infusion to tighten up those vile, facial flaws. The infusion, which is made from the plant's roots, has a strong astringent quality.

The "berries" are boiled for about five minutes to obtain candle wax. When the broth has cooled, the wax is skimmed off. According to one account, a bushel of the tiny "berries" will yield up to four pounds of wax.

I leave that chore for others and purchase my candles in a candles-and-such gift shop. I know exactly what I want when I enter the store, but pretend to be uncertain of what to purchase.

"Just looking around a bit for now, thank you." I wanted to get in as much free candle aroma sniffing as I could. Some blueberry scented candles did tempt me to make an impulse purchase, but I didn't.

I left the gift shop with my bayberry candle purchase, the thick, long lasting sort, happy as a myrtle warbler—or something akin to that.

NO FEAR FOR TOMORROW

Cherry Pyron

Anna was ticking off the precautions John should heed after his first chemo treatment when his question of "How will I know if I have a fever?" stopped her short. Same feeling I had to quickly swallow when a few weeks earlier he had asked, "What's an oncologist?"

The second day after an X-ray had shown a large mass in John's upper chest, I drove to Memphis to a writer's conference. Early Saturday morning, alone in the car, about an hour into my trip, still numb after two quick days jammed with medical consultations, blood tests, one biopsy and CT scans – the first tears came hard and fast. They began to wash out some of the fear of what lay ahead, the anger that this was happening to John and not to me, and grief so deep the sobs that began as howls tapered into moans. With body rocking, they became a quiet wailing, the lament a mother experiences when she loses part of her heart.

This couldn't be cancer and certainly not be happening to 20-year-old John – but I knew that would be the diagnosis. Yet there was no dark hopeless feeling. Healing would come.

Death holds less fear for me since we lost John's lifetime pal in a car accident two years ago. Whenever John was not home when I got ready to go to bed, I would lie awake with visions of a crashed vehicle upside down, wheels still spinning, panicked, trying not to see what was so vivid in my head, but knowing the possibility of experiencing a horrible reality I'd already known at Dylan's death. One night in a true terror sweat, I screamed in my head, "No!!" – and with an unexplained, powerful quickness, the spinning fatal image vanished, and I couldn't bring it back, even if I tried, and still can't.

We have to let go of our fear so that fear's grip on us is broken. Then we can begin to trust what has happened, what is happening, so that healing can come.

If I could release one terror, I knew I could do the same with this new burden. Still, in the next five weeks before the diagnosis of Hodgkin's lymphoma, the tears of anxiety and fear continued in fits, sometimes like spring showers, more often like strong summer downpours, boiling up quickly and flooding with intensity.

Resolve also washed through in those days, bringing a sense of peace. The only approach we had was asking what could we do and trusting knowledgeable, compassionate people to guide us through the coming months.

John's final chemo treatment will come two days after Easter, and we're all acknowledging the significance of that timing – at the beginning of the season of rebirth, new life, hope's victory after three days of utter darkness. We do not know the future but we see today with eyes not so often flooded by tears but rather cleared to realize the gift of every single day, unhampered by trying to be in control. Jesus talked about our anxiety and living for tomorrow in Matthew's Gospel, reminding us that worrying about tomorrow is foolish, that today's trouble is enough for today.

What comes tomorrow, the possibility of death, the certainty of death at some time, holds darkness and yet also holds light. We realize no matter how tightly or closely we hold those so dear to our hearts, our claim is tenuous and we can do nothing to add a single minute to any of our times. So we release our fear, our powerlessness, in faith, sometimes peeling away just one finger at a time. A smile begins again to play across our damp faces and the gentle wind from the love of a Father who was willing to give up his own child dries our tears.

And healing will indeed come.

Drawing by Christina Brooks

YOUNG WRITERS

IN DREAMS

If I knew my way back home
to the place where I belong
I would be there with you.
On a distant hillside you dream
of all the things you have seen
and the things in between.

Tonight I won't find peace
because the miles bar me from sleep
and I find myself lost in the dark of night
with a tired resolution to find my way.
Still I fight off sleep because I'll see another day.
But I'll never see it quite the same
because nothing is ever forever
but everything is forever unchanged.

Maybe I'm what isn't the same
but I will return to the place where I belong
I will be there with you.
On a green hillside we'll dream
of all the things we've seen
and the things in between.

Melissa Taylor

BLAST THAT GUY SHAKESPEARE;
HE MAKES THE REST OF US LOOK BAD

I don't understand
Nor do I comprehend
How poets can write such beauty
In such a structured form of written hand

I tried, God help me, I tried
To write a Shakespearian sonnet
But how can one match his mind
Without losing their own in the process?

I suppose one must be highly skilled
In the art of melody and speech
To compose that blasted iambic poetry
Yet have their goals still reached

But my artistic mind isn't built that way
Though I yearn to be poet in part
As you can see, this really isn't my forte
So I suppose I'll stick with art...

Laurie Skelton

Drawing by Patrick Banks

Drawing by Tommie Franklin

KITE

Flying, sailing through the air
Soaring, gliding, floating where
Enjoyable, colorful, dash and hover
Crashing to the ground by the wind

Christopher Watts

SOMETIMES

Sometimes I feel as if I want to fly away
From all my troubles and fears,
To wipe away all my tears
And just fly up, up and away into the sky.
To go so high where there is no sorrow and pain,
Where everyone is happy, so happy
Laughter fills the air and my hair is waving in the wind
If there is such a place with all that warm happy embrace
We would have nothing to work on here
So although I fear that the world is full of hate,
Maybe we can change that fate
We can keep working on that warm, happy place
Right here !

Aishah EI-Akkari

Eye-poem by Ticara Gailliard

Eye-poem by Bethany Byrd

DOMINO

Katie Williams

I have a special pet. You could call her strange. She doesn't have two heads or anything like that but she's a cow. Actually she's a heifer. I show her in livestock shows all around the area. We keep her in a pen, and I have to walk her every day for thirty minutes to keep her from getting fat before I show her. At first, I started walking her in the driveway and in my grandmother's pasture, but after a while she got bored and would stop every once and a while and moo as loud as she could. So, we started walking her on the road. Then, everybody knew that I had a pet cow.

After awhile though, everybody got used to my pet cow. It was just like seeing a car going down the road, no big deal. The man that runs the RV place in our town, Denny Durham, said a woman from Missouri came to look at an

RV, and she saw me walking my heifer. She thought that was the funniest thing she had ever seen. Denny said he told her that he never thought about it being weird or funny, they were used to it now.

Once a man who lives down the street from my grandmother asked us if we were walking my heifer all summer.. We said yes, and he said good. He told us he had a group from Canada coming down for a wedding in July. He wanted me to be sure and walk her because, in his words, "They ain't never seen nothing like that before." People all the way to Canada have heard about my pet heifer.

I guess you could say that my heifer is the center of attention. Kids will come up to me and ask if they can pet her. Of course, I let them. My heifer is very special to me and very special to our town.

WOLF

Wolf I followed
You hunting your prey

    This is your job
    To do for the day

Wolf I saw you
Howl at the moon

    I heard you so
    I'll be there soon

Wolf I found you
Starting to munch

Your pups are hungry
    They want their lunch.

Courtney Watts

Eye-Poem by Sarah Nolen

From the sketchbook of Erwin Doege

SALUTING FLORIDA
WRITERS AND ARTISTS

Sketch by Bonnie Warner

In my flowerbed
a hummingbird, here and there—
everywhere then gone

Bonnie L. Warner

MAN OF MANY FACETS

Man of many facets,
like a diamond iridescent in the sunlight,
each polished surface reflecting
yet another aspect of personality.

Romanticist and pragmatist
letting imagination run wild
but continually pricking dream balloons
with the sharp probe of realism.

Catalyst and alchemist;
Influencing reactions
and with a magic power
transmuting baser things of life into pure gold.

Architect and iconoclast;
contriving wondrous structures for the future
while shattering gilded images
of falseness and pretense.

Laborer and troubadour;
plodding at the daily tasks
so necessary to exist
yet bringing music and poetry to lift the heart.

Sensualist and idealist;
satisfying passions of the body
but reaching ever upward
toward visions of the soul.

Historian and prophet;
drawing judgments from the past
predicting unerringly
the future fulfillment of our destinies.

Through the years the contrasts
become more sharply defined:
I turn the precious stone to reveal
new, exciting facets for my ever-searching eyes.

Pearl S. Lupin

ANGER

I have seen its leading
edge. How it ripped
the roots, unhinged
the roof, collapsed
my home. Escape
routes were flooded
with torrential
rage. Now, because the sky turned
blue, you think the worst
is past. But behind this calm
eye, winds are building.
Left unsheltered, on flat, low
lying lands,
brace yourself. Here comes
the trailing
            edge.

Anna DeMay

FADED PHOTOGRAPHS
(My Grandfather, Robert D. Carter)

He came to Florida in 1915,
bringing his young family with him;
wife in white lawn and wide-brimmed
hat, son and daughter - left behind another infant son,
returned to the earth of his native North Carolina.

They found a homestead lot still remaining;
lived in a tent three feet off the ground
until their home took shape. An engineer by training,
he found his heart's occupation in the dairy farm
and groves that shaped and grew with his direction.
His wife a soul mate pioneer, kept wandering cattle off
and family close, as she tended her home,
her garden and her chickens. Each family on its own
in daily work, community was a blessing;
the grace of church and town and neighbors.
When a car passed on their quiet gravel road, they
knew who it was and where they were going.

With transit and rod, he
marked out the lines for canals and roads,
bumping out to the swamp in mule-drawn wagons,
his crew dressed in sun-hats and khakis,
high-laced boots to foil the water moccasins,
smoky fires to keep away mosquitoes.
Only eyes to fend off alligators.
The fertile land waited with its
abundant water, to grow vast groves
of citrus, Indian River gold.
As their lives and trees flourished
in Florida's damp and sandy soil,
another son's spirit rose like smoke,
a sacrificial offering to the all-absorbing earth.
The boy and girl grew sturdy as the richest grove,

strong and green toward abundant fruits,
as their roots thrust deep into the Florida earth.

Memories, like photographs, fade.
His mark on the earth remains.
His canals drained space for cattle, groves, and houses;
his roads provided access. When he died,
his honor lay forever in the fruition of his plans, in
trees and homes, in the artistry of people
who sought and seek the richness of this land.

Frances W. Muir

cats sit and wait
can opens   eyes open
supper time

Frances W. Muir

SOLITUDE

Gray clouds. Streaks of sad gray rain
trickle through shivering leaves.
Walking under weeping trees
Beside a dark gray river,
one person, shadowed in black,
carries a red umbrella.

Frances W. Muir

NIGHT DIVE

Water black abyss glistening
shimmering and reflecting
our so gently rocking
fragile craft

sending tiny rippling lines from
hull mirrored deep in inky
fluid illuminated on the
edge of not seen

splashing now shatters quiet
eyes turn see diamonds in
spattering water drops

reflecting glare to us swaying
in time with restless sea
luminescence absorbed

wondering what broke noisily
from depths to leap what
burst upward glistening
then thrust down

time passes filigreed clouds
reflect on surrounding
surface beneath
which we'll

soon be as boat rolls above
sliding up and down
ebony slopes
softly

C. E. Larsen

I HAVE WORN THIS SHIRT

I have worn this shirt of yours until
It is not flannel anymore, but
A loose veil thin as my sleep.
Through its threads I can already see
Snow light and rain frail as fog, falling.
Your shirt--beaten on midnight rocks,
Rinsed in brine and vinegar, dried in sandy
Winds that blow from a stone sun—
Has almost given up its little ghost.
It hangs on my body as though it knows
I am not you; as though it remembers
Better than I do the feel and fullness
Of your arms and shoulders; as though
It would weave into new cloth, if
Your apparition appeared in my doorway.

When I have mended your garment until
It no longer will mend, before it has
At last become a shirt of air, I shall
Cut one piece to fold and put away beneath
The silence of your socks; its buttons
Made of bone will lie in a metal box
Rattling with fake companions, blue and brown
And plastic pearl, hide themselves when I look
To see if they are still there or missing
By those secrets only bone and buttons know.
The rest will be rags for dusting webs from
This dark and spidered furniture ... if ever
I come to caring about dust again.

June Owens

From *Pegasus,* and author's book-length collection, *Tree Line*, 1999

Photo by L. Boulton

THE WALL

In memory of those who did not return
from Vietnam, and in honor of those who did

I am the granite Wall
Projecting majestically
Toward the open heavens
For all who come to me

I beckon you in the sunshine
I wait for others in the rain
Each name engraved in tenderness
To help release the pain

You kneel or stand, eyes searching
I sense your longing to speak
Hoping to leave years of grief behind
You lay flowers and souvenirs at my feet

I welcome the curious and broken hearted
And comfort all those who come in pain
To read names of veterans who sacrificed
With hands trembling you trace one warrior's name

I hear the messages you whisper
Sad memories are revived I know
Let me divide your grief in half
Take my strength home when you go
If I could speak I would tell you
To cry, then dry your eyes by and by
They are heroes, be proud, then remember
You can let go, at last, to say good-bye.

Laurie Boulton

BEACH RUIN

Steel fingers stretching
Growing from the dunes
Tranquility uprooted
Concrete blobs encroaching
Palm fronds share salty air
Nature's playground spoiled.

Laurie Boulton

Photo by L. Boulton

on a beach boardwalk
homeless man prepares his meal
no where else to go.

Laurie Boulton

ASHES TO ASHES

Eyes like windows blocked by weathered shutters,
Caught the light so dim in that day.
Swirling clouds crawled by barely moving
Like spiders cautious to alert their prey.
Sounds, like the melancholy moaning of cows
Newly separated from their calves,
Filled even the corners of the building
like pieces of hay trapped, lying straw-like
and swept into the corners with dust
that had drifted in on an incessantly sifting wind.
Feelings numb like cold, hard, twisted metal machinery,

lay exposed, without cushion,
rent open as if by sharp-toothed rodents
looking for a place to nest.
There was no rest.
The smell was seeping in musty and pungent
like a ravenous candle flame licking into the creosol coating
of some incensed cherished wood treasure.
The end was near.
The heat drew closer.
Eyes darted in flashes, owl-like in intensity.
The lone dove cooing near the tree nearby
did little to smother the tension.
The planks creaked like ball joints popping.
A sound like an engine grinding moved closer
with a thunderous clatter,
to hang like an ominous insect looking for a lifeline.
The earth shook as if violated.
The clawing tooth bit down tearing the heart out,
The taste of defeat and grief filled the air.
Weak with years and worn by use,
she could no longer stand.
No shelter here.
Exposed and vulnerable, all became smoke.
Like a spirit yielding to a greater power,
The soul of ash fed the fire as the old barn wood lit up the
sky.

Meg Roman

ILLUMINATION

With radiant light
Lanterns lit like sleepless stars
Set the sky aglow.

Susanne Leeds

On steaming highway
Perched atop telephone wires
Birds steering traffic.

Susanne Leeds

DEGREES OF POVERTY
Miriam Doege

"I'd jump if I had something to stood on," a friend and mentor often said to me. It always made me laugh, bringing the image of someone jumping up and down getting nowhere, but the sobering thought followed. We have to have a starting place. He also said, "There are only two things to remember for financial security, either spend less than you make or make more than you spend." Succinct and true if you are making anything.

Poverty, in its ugly, debilitating form, carries the hopelessness of not "having something to stood on." The man on the corner with a sign saying, "I'll work for food," is a rude awakener to reality.

There are degrees of poverty, not all so stark. The first definition in my Webster's dictionary reads, "a lack of money or material possessions."

On the fringe of the Beatnik era of the 50's, a lot of people embraced a certain type of poverty for the sake of art or artistic life-styles. The Hippies of the 70's did the same. Well-bred kids in forty dollar T-shirts, sporting poverty.

My frustrated artist (supporting the family in architecture) husband and I never thought of our selves as "poor." We did have little appreciation for material things and spent most of our income to "support our habit" of art. In 1958, we embarked on an adventure of poverty. We would sell our house in Miami, Florida, move to New York City, and find cheap living quarters. He would devote his entire energy to painting, until the money ran out from the sale of the house. Our children, six and four, would either be in school or home with their full-time artist father; I would find part time work to make the house money last longer. We were excited.

Half filled boxes, rolls of canvas, art supplies, books, music, lined the walls. Our junky furniture waited for the Salvation Army to pick up. Both kids came down with the chicken-pox. The real estate "For Sale" sign planted in the front yard stayed put, in spite of chicken-pox.

"Hello, have you folks had chicken-pox?" I asked, with the brightest smile I could muster up.

What a mess. Both kids covered in pox, noses running, bedroom littered with toys, books, anything to keep their minds off itching—and a fragmented Mom. The poor prospective buyers were somewhat distracted. I heard a lot of,

"Hmm. Oh yes. Hmm. Well I think we've seen enough. Thank you very much."

One day, a panel truck drove slowly past, turned and backed into our carport. Two guys got out, knocked on the utility room door.

"We'd like to see your house," one of the men said when I went to the door.

"Well, it's a mess. My children have chicken-pox. Is that a problem?" They said no and I let them in.

"We're checking out houses. If we like 'em we'll bring our wives later." They made small talk, really looking around.

"What are all these pictures? You do 'em?"

"No, my husband is a painter. Kids, get back in bed, I'll bring you some soup in a bit.

"Too bad you packed up your TV," the taller guy said, eyeing the boxes, "Little kiddies could watch cartoons."

"Oh, we don't have a television set."

"Hmm. These pictures look pretty good. They worth anything, Little Lady?"

"Some day, we hope. You know what they say about starving artists. They have to die before their paintings are worth anything," I said.

"Well, I think we've seen enough, uh, Joe, what you say?"

"Yeah, we'll tell the wives. Good luck, Lady. Hope the little kiddies get over them poxes." I watched the van pull out my drive and accelerate down the street. Sometime later, between chores, it dawned on me. Those men meant to rob me. I broke out in a cold sweat. The children and I could have been hurt.

"You dummy!" I said out loud, "How stupid can you be? Backed into my carport. Neighbors couldn't see them haul out everything they wanted..."

Laughter built up and gurgled out with the thought: "There wasn't anything they wanted. They even felt sorry for us!"

The children, peeking from the bedroom, laughed too. Must have thought things were pretty good with Mom so happy. I hugged them close.

"How about some ice-cream and a story? Forget the soup." They clapped their hands.

Poverty can have advantages. Depends on the degree.

From the sketchbook of Erwin Doege

Pencolo Beach by Barbara Abbott

Sunset on the St. John's River by Aishah EI-Akkari

ROCKS!

William B. Caudle II

"Rocks!" That was what he saw as he looked towards the rivulet, and what he saw translated to what he said, but with more enthusiasm.

It was incredible, he thought, that so many rocks had been gathered in one place and seemed ensconced in one field. "There are so many rocks in this state, it must be the seed-bed for all the rocks in the world," he said to himself. His frustration was escalating.

He let out a long and vocal "harumph!" in exasperation. "Cheri," he yelled up the stairs. The release seemed to bring him down a notch. He realized it wasn't so much a field as it was just a large yard. Nor were these rocks as large as he had imagined. Some were no more than mere pebbles, but the largest would put a good-sized nick in a lawn mower blade; that is, if he hadn't the good sense not to mow the yard.

"Cheri," he yelled up the stairs again. He heard her walking from the bedroom towards the hall that led to the stairs up which he had called.

"What, Dear?" she answered.

"Do we have any gas?" he yelled again, even though she had moved closer.

"I don't know," she said calmly and in a normal voice. "Why don't you look in the gas can?"

"Can't find it," he mumbled, not wanting her to hear his answer.

"What?" she asked, having not heard what he said.

He didn't respond.

"Oh, I see it," he answered without having to admit to his mumbling.

"What?" she was louder now, as her irritation of having been taken from her "duties" upstairs increased. He could hear her coming down the stairs.

"Nothing," he yelled. She did not always hear what he said, and he hated repeating what he thought should have been heard in the first place. He thought she might be in need of a hearing aid. He didn't like to yell because of the strain. His voice was naturally soft, and he did not like to strain it. He preferred to think of her "deafness" as the reason he had to yell.

"Why do you want the gas?" she was standing at the foot of the stairs. She had always been solicitous of his every need, and this behavior was only an example.

"Huh? Oh, I was thinking of cutting the grass. But there's a problem – rocks!" He moved towards where he had spotted the red gas can.

Nothing was where it should be, with good reason. They had just moved into a brand-new home in Summertown, Tennessee.

"What about the rocks?" she asked. She had not noticed the rocks for the verdant green of the grass and the blossoms on the dogwood.

"Huh? Oh," he repeated. "The rocks are big enough to make dents in the mower blades. I'm concerned about them," he told her.

"So why are you going to mow the rocks?" she queried him, knowing he must have a reason. He usually did.

"I'm not. I'm just making sure we have the gas when I do mow. *And*," he said emphatically, "I'm not going to mow the rocks!"

"What about the rocks?" she asked, even though she felt it was none of her concern. His domain included the rocks. Hers was the house.

"We're going to pick them up," he glowed over his shoulder. She noticed the uplifting eyebrows and the smile on his face. It made her suspicious.

"We?" She was now attentive.

"Yeah. I'll need your help. You can pull the cart while we walk over the yard to get the large ones out."

"Why can't you do this?"

"Romance," he smiled again, without further explanation. He thought she might catch on.

"Romance?" she stared at him, as her voice had grown noticeably more irritated. "How can picking up rocks be romantic?" She was fuming, near tears. She liked flowers and a candle-lit dinner and good, slow, soft music. That was romantic.

"You don't care about me anymore. You don't care about romance. You don't know the meaning of the word." The tears began to run down her cheek. "Our marriage must be over if you think that rocks are romantic." She was snuffling and dabbing at the tears and her nose with a tissue she had kept in her pocket twice too long.

He looked at her, puzzled that his idea of romance would brings such a flood of remonstrance.

"Rocks aren't romantic, Hon," he said quietly.

"But you said they were."

"No, not the rocks. I didn't say the rocks were romantic. I meant for you to understand that working together is romantic. Not the rocks."

'Oh," she looked sheepish and snuffled her last, dabbing the last of her tears away. "Oh," she said again.

"I meant that we could overcome this problem – the rocks – together, and we could spend some time solving one of our little problems while we are spending time together. That's the romance." He smiled the impish smile that he knew she loved.

"Oh," she said once more. "Okay, I thought you just wanted me to be a mule. You're always wanting me to work more than I do. Well, I do work hard . . . for me."

"But," he started to interject. She continued wanting to get the thought out before it fled of its own accord.

"You don't tell me enough that you love me and how much. We don't go out enough and . . . and . . . "

He knew it was time to intervene. "But," he persisted, "work is what we are here to do. It's a means to perfection. God, our Heavenly Father, gave us, His sons and daughters, a gift in work. He wants us to learn by the problems He gives us."

"Or that we create ourselves," she added.

"The rocks are problems we can work through. And if we work through them together, we will find success."

"Success?" she asked perplexed. "What kind of success? You mean about the rocks?"

"No, – well, yes – that, too. But more at overcoming a problem – any problem. *And*," he emphasized, "perfecting a relationship with someone. After all, isn't that more important that rocks?" He smiled, and they picked up the gas can together.

Ponce Inlet Lighthouse by Bonnie L. Warner

PRESSURE IN PARADISE

Audrey Cooke

God created Adam and Eve and saw what he made was good. One day, early on, during His usual morning tutorial, He told them to pay attention.

"Stop fooling around," He said. "This is important. I want you to realize that I have given you a very special gift." Eve stopped braiding Adam's hair with red berries and Adam stopped picking his toes. They both looked up at God adoringly.

"What's the gift, God?" Adam asked.

"I have given you..." God paused for dramatic effect before adding, "perfect blood pressure, 120/70. And I want you to keep it that way."

"How do we do that, God?" Eve asked.

God told them to get plenty of exercise, drink a lot of water from the crystal clear springs and eat all the right food from anywhere in the garden—except from the you-know-what-tree. "And especially, God thundered, "avoid hypertension."

"What's hypertension, God?" Adam asked.

"You'll know it if it hits you," said God. "Avoid it. It's a killer." Then He added, "Because your perfect blood pressure is a very special gift which I want you to pass on to your children and their children, you will be subjected, from time to time, to random tests."

"O. K., God." Adam and Eve replied in unison

Their lesson over, they merrily romped around in the garden, eating strawberries and naming the animals. Suddenly, a strange, unfamiliar sound resonated behind them. They spun around. Hisssss...Hisssss. The sound was getting louder. Coming closer. Then they saw the creature. Undulating, like an endless, shiny black river through the tall, green grasses, it approached them. They froze. The creature slithered to a stop about three feet in front of them, raised its ugly head and hissed again.

"We should get out of here," Eve whispered to Adam. "Look, I've got goose bumps all over. I'm shivering. I think I've got hypertension."

"Me, too," Adam whispered back. "I've broken into my first cold sweat. Don't worry, Eve, I'll scare him off."

Mopping his brow with the back of his hand, he stepped forward an inch or two and looked down at the scary intruder. "Who are you?" he asked, sounding braver than he felt. "What do you want?"

The snake, for that's who it was, arched its neck and hissed again, trying to muffle the ss's so the greeting would sound more like Hi! "Why, I've been sent to take your blood pressure," the creature said

"A random test?" Eve gasped. "So soon?"

"That's right," said the snake. "A random test. Ladies first! Come here, Eve, and kneel down close beside me."

Shuddering with fright, Eve did as she was told. Out of nowhere, it seemed, the snake's endless speckled tail suddenly appeared and wrapped itself round and round Eve's upper arm. Squeezing. Squeezing. Eve let out a shriek and fainted on the spot.

Uncoiling its tail from Eve's arm, the snake nodded at Adam. "Your turn."

Too dazed to protest, Adam stumbled forward and fell to his knees. This time, the tail swung out it the opposite direction and spun itself round and round Adam's upper arm. And squeezed and squeezed. Adam clenched his teeth. Finally, finally, the tail loosened itself from Adam's arm and flipped itself back to where it belonged, hidden in the high grasses. Adam collapsed on the ground beside Eve.

The snake began to make gyrating motions with its neck and kept at it until it made itself very tall. Then it let out a loud and long hiss. Adam and Eve came out of their comas and looked up to find the snake glowering down at them.

"You have both failed the Blood Pressure Test,' the snake announced. "No more 120/70 for you. Your numbers are off the chart. God's not going to like that one bit. You're in really big trouble."

"Oh, we know! We know," wailed Eve. "He warned us about that only this morning."

"It's all your fault, "Adam told the snake. "You scared us. We never had any hypertension till you showed up."

"I apologize if I frightened you," said the snake, swaying back and forth the whole time. "I certainly didn't mean to. However, being an expert on medical matters, I know of an antidote that could cure your problem."

"You do?" Adam and Eve were back on their knees, looking up beseechingly into the yellow eyes of this strange creature.

"Yes," said the snake, now gyrating downward. "All you have to do to get your blood pressure back to its original, perfect level is eat the fruit—skin, core, pits and all—of a certain tree here in the garden."

"Which one?" Eve wanted to know.

The snake lifted and twirled its tail, which then shot out like an arrow—pointing to the Tree of Knowledge of Good and Evil.

"Oh, we can't go near that one," said Adam. "That one's off limits. It's out of the question."

"It's the only cure," said the snake, now level with the ground. "And you better be quick about it before God sends someone else to check your blood pressure. Or comes to check it Himself." Letting out a low hiss, it swished itself around and disappeared into the tall grasses.

What a quandary! Well, of course, they ate the apples. Skin, seeds, core and all. Right off the Tree of Knowledge of Good and Evil. When they'd finished swallowing the last forbidden bite, they had jangled nerves, stomach aches and worse.

"Oh, God!" Adam moaned, writhing on the ground.

"Oh, Adam!" came the voice of God, thundering in the clouds. "You've been a very naughty, little man."

"It's all the snake's fault." Adam cried. "He scared us and made our blood pressure go off the charts."

"But the apple, Adam," said God. "You and Eve shouldn't have eaten the apples."

"But the snake said it was the only cure for our hypertension," Eve blubbered between sobs.

"And was it?" asked God. "After eating the forbidden fruit, did you feel tranquil and serene?"

"Oh, no!" they both wailed, doubling over.

"Your fear of the snake would subside once the serpent tired of taunting you," said God. "Your blood pressure would soon resume its normal balance. But, after breaking your trust with Me and realizing your guilt, that's when the numbers went off the chart. That's when your blood pressure started to skyrocket. As a result, your descendents, in the billions, will come into this world victims of high blood pressure problems.

"Instead of romping around in the garden like you two, enjoying the fruits of the earth, your children must watch what they eat, pay enormous sums for medications— even travel to faraway lands to procure them at prices they can afford. Hypertension, instead of being a rare exception, will become the norm, leading to wars, murders and road rage. People will die by the millions, of heart disease and stroke."

"You two have been very, very bad children. Go to your room. Wherever you can find it. Outside the garden."

God shook His head in puzzlement, and thought, What a dopey thing to do—listening to a snake!

WHEN THERE'S NOTHING TO DO

Dorothy Hatfield

Sarah slammed her fist against the steering wheel as the cars in front of her slowed to a stop. For the past hour, a wreck on Interstate 40 had caused traffic to creep along in the 90-degree heat. She glanced at her watch as the pulled off Exit 12 in Memphis. 7:00pm already! She would spend the night here. After Nancy's call about their dad, Sarah had left Nashville right after lunch, planning to stay over in Little Rock. From there, the drive to Dallas was easy. Now with these delays, rather than arriving tomorrow in the early afternoon, she would be fighting rush hour traffic.

Sarah dropped her bag in the motel room and sat on the edge of the bed. Why was she making the twelve-hour trip to see her dad? Their time together was always spent laughing and joking or having a dinner of Dad's favorite chicken-fried steak. Would the joy still be there? Or would future uncertainties cast a cloud? With a sigh, she let her body fall back across the bed and she lay there, staring at the ceiling. She thought again of her sister's words, "Congestive heart failure...maybe six more months...down hill all the way from here." Sarah tried to rationalize; Dad's 80 years old. He's had a good life. But, he's *Dad*! He's still bright and wise and useful. Whatever will I do without him?

"I'm coming," Sarah told Nancy.

"Fine, come on," Nancy's voice sounded flat. "But there's nothing you can do here."

Nothing she could do? She was Managing Partner of a major investment firm. She took charge of complicated situations every day. Through hard work, she had established herself in a highly competitive business. She was at the peak of her earning power, fully vested in a comfortable retirement plan. Nothing she could *do?* She shut her eyes tightly to hold back the threatening tears. "Stop it," she said out loud. She rose quickly, deciding to go for a swim before supper.

On top of her swimsuit lay the Bible Dad had given her for Christmas nearly twenty years ago. She had hurriedly tossed it in the suitcase just before fastening the lid. Now, she picked it up. Tucked between the pages was the daily Bible reading guide she followed occasionally. Her hectic life did not allow time to read every day. Now, she opened the book. Maybe there would be some answers in the scriptures.

Slowly, Sarah read from Mark 14: the story of the woman from Bethany who anointed Jesus with perfume. The disciples scolded her for being so wasteful, but Jesus understood her gift, saying, *"She has done a beautiful thing to me... You will not always have me. She did what she could... to prepare my body for burial. ...wherever the gospel is preached, what she has done will also be told..."*

As she read, tears filled her eyes and dropped on the pages, blurring the words. *"...She did what she could... prepare my body for burial. You will not always have me."* Sarah had hoped for comfort. Instead, the words seemed to accent her grief.

She shut the book. "I will not cry," she said, snatching her swimsuit from the bag. "I need a swim."

Sarah was glad to find the pool almost deserted. The man sitting in the lounge chair was fully clothed, obviously not planning to swim. A woman wearing a floppy hat gave him a wave as she walked through the gate of the pool area. Sarah sank into a nearby chair, twisting her hair into a knot and fastening it with a clip.

"She wanted to come to Memphis to see Graceland," the man said. Sarah looked up. There was no one else the man could be talking to, so Sarah asked politely if they had enjoyed the tour of Elvis' home.

"I don't care much about that sort of thing, but she wanted to come. So, we came over yesterday and went to Graceland today." He gazed at the woman as she walked to the edge of the pool and bent to test the water. "She has a doctor's appointment in Nashville tomorrow, but she wanted to come to Memphis first." Sarah did not want to seem rude, but was not sure why he was telling her this.

The woman walked to the chair beside the man, took off her robe and kicked out of her sandals. She removed the hat. With one look, Sarah knew the reason for the trip to Nashville. The wispy tufts of hair, either falling out or growing in, the evidence of the aftermath of chemotherapy, explained it all. The woman lowered herself into the pool and floated on her back. She closed her eyes, completely relaxed, a faint smile playing around the corners of her mouth. Sarah watched the woman move in the water, unable to look away from the expression of pure enjoyment.

While his wife swam, the man told Sarah they were to see a doctor at Vanderbilt Medical Center to talk about the possibility of a bone marrow transplant. Sarah murmured some reply about the doctors at Vanderbilt being wondrously wise and assured the man his wife would have the best of care. But, Sarah was thinking of 1981: Dad and Mother making the weekly trips to Dallas for the treatments that had left Mother nauseated and weak. Dad would find a new restaurant to try, a movie they had never seen, or something special to do to make the day seem lighter. He still loved to tell about seeing *"On Golden Pond,"* featuring two favorite actors, now seniors also. They had sat in the theater holding hands, thinking of the Hepburn and Fonda of their courting days. Mother always went along with Dad's plans, enjoying the sights, smells, and sounds of each experience while it lasted. Dad relished these outings he planned for them together. It was something he could do for her.

The woman climbed out of the pool and toweled herself dry as she and her husband carried on an animated conversation about where they should have dinner. Sarah watched as they walked through the gate, hand in hand, laughing softly.

She leaned back in the lounge chair. As the last rays of sun reflected off the pool, she said a silent prayer for the man and his wife. She added a thank you for her parents and the love they had shared. She thought again of the woman from Bethany, showing Jesus her love in the best way she knew how. *"She did what she could." When There's Nothing to Do.*

Sarah had her answer. What do you do when there's nothing to do? You do what you can. You show your love: lavishly, as the woman from Bethany, or simply, as Dad and the man at the pool. You give a lovely gift, you see a movie, you go to Graceland, you take your dad out for chicken-fried steak.

Photo by Neal Hogenbirk

MEET THE JUDGES

Jennifer Jensen is a former attorney in Memphis, TN, who is now attending seminary. She tries to write a different haiku each day. She has appeared in many issues of *Grandmother Earth.*

Frank Reed Nichols, Memphis, TN, is an award winning poet and novelist, and a retired architect from Memphis, TN. His latest novel, *The Knell* is about the ramifications of euthanasia. He has been interviewed on the Library Channel in Memphis. He is now working on *Uncle Newt* and *The Gold Mine*, both sagas based on the Nichols family.

Clovita Rice, Little Rock, AR, was editor of *Voices International* and Director of the AR Writers Confernce for many years. She is working on a collection of poetry and prose.

Dorothy Bullard Tacker, Tyronza, AR, judged the Florida contest which was given in memory of her parents. Although this is her first time as a judge, she is an avid reader having read the published work of her daughter, Frances Cowden, for almost 40 years and including all of the issues of *Grandmother Earth* as well as many issues of *Voices International* and *Tennessee Voices.*

MEET THE STAFF

Frances Brinkley Cowden is founder of Grandmother Earth and Life Press. Grandmother Earth won the 1995 Business Environmental Award given by the city of Germantown, TN. Cowden received the Purple Iris Award in 2000 for outstanding contribution to the community though her publishing and the Life Press writing conference. The Iris Awards are co-sponsored by the Memphis branch of the National Organization of Business Women. In 2001 she was selected as one of the 50 Women who Make a Difference by *Memphis Woman Magazine.*

Frances Darby contributed to *Our Golden Thread,* and has work in all of the *Grandmother Earth* series. She is the widow of the late Rev. James W. Darby, a United Methodist minister. She is an editorial assistant for *Grandmother Earth.*

Lorraine Smith is a English and Spanish teacher retired from Germantown High School and active in the PST and NLAPW, Memphis Branch.

Patricia Smith is editor of and critic for *Grandmother Earth* and other GEC and Life Press publications. Her Life Press Conference workshop has been popular each year with both beginning and seasoned writers. She is an officer of the NLAPW, Chickasaw Branch and PST.

E. Marcelle Zarshenas, a Memphis attorney, has helped with the editing and judging of Grandmother Earth publications since its beginning in 1993.

CONTRIBUTORS

Common abbreviations used: PST, Poetry Society of Tennessee;
NLAPW, National League of American Pen Women;
National Association of State Poetry Societies;
FSPA, Florida State Poetry Association.

Adams, Burlington, Burlington, CA is a frequent contributor to *Grandmother Earth.*

Jane E. Allen, Wetumpka, AL, enjoys writing fiction, nonfiction, and poetry. Her works have been included in *Progressive Farmer*; *Ordinary and Sacred As Blood*: *Alabama Women speak*; *Grandmother Earth; Tough Times, Strong Women; The Alalitcom; 103Rosie the Riveter Stories;* and *Mystery Time.*

Therese Arceneaux, Lafayette, LA , has been published in over 30 magazines—several awards from *The Lyric,* including The Lyric Memorial Prize for 1999. Third Place Winner in *The Comstock Review's* national competition in 1997. Editor's Choice Award in *Grandmother Earth III.*   Chapbook: *Where Music Lives,* Chicago Spectrum Press, 1999.

Auguste R. Black, Huntsville, AL, was a big winner at the 2002 Life Press Christian Writers Conference. She has won previously in the Grandmother Earth Awards. She writes children's books.

Theresa Brown, Louisville, KY, has been published in Misnomer and Across the University, an anthology of North American poets. She has also won prizes in the Green River Writer's Poetry Contest.

Florence Bruce, Memphis, TN, a retired medical transcriptionist writes and edits for local physicians. She has won numerous awards including *Grandmother Earth's* top prose award in 1998.

Marcia Camp, Little Rock, AR, won the Sybil Nash Abrams Award in 1984 and 1998. Her poetry and prose appear in both regional and national publications. Her self-help book, *You Can't Leave Till You do the Paperwork: Matters of Life and Death*, is currently in bookstores.

Bettye Kramer Cannizzo, Decatur, AL, a Mississippi Yankee, has been published in *Grandmother Earth, The Elk River Review, Alalitcom, Alabama Horizons,* and *NFSPS's Anthology.* She is a member of the Alabama State Poetry Society, Alabama Conclave of Writers, the Huntsville branch of NLAPW and the Mountain Valley Poets. Bettye is Vice President for the ASPS and secretary of the Alabama State Association of NLAPW.

Neil Chandler, Mountain Home, AR, lives in the Ozarks where golf and singing compete with writing. His book, *The Last Decade of Innocence* contains stories from small-town America.

Arla Clemons, Las Crosse, WI, is a retired physical education teacher, now pursuing her writing career. She has been published in the *Wisconsin Poets' Calendar, Touchstone, Promise Magazine, Grandmother Earth and Splintered Sunlight* (Anthology 2000 published by the Arizona State Poetry Society). She has won awards in Sky Blue Waters Poetry Contests and Sinipee Writers' Contest. "A day without writing is a day that has lost some of its memory."

James B. Copening, Ft. Smith, AR, was born in eastern Kansas. Semi-retired at 81, he works part-time in sales. Credits include *Byline* and *Thema.* He won a first place last year for prose in *Grandmother Earth.* He started writing 10 years ago after attending a junior college writing class.

John Crawford, Professor of English Literature at Henderson State University, Arkedelphia, AR, is also a noted pianist.

Frieda Beasley Dorris, Memphis, TN, is one of the originators of the Dorsimbra poetry form. A past president of the Poetry Society of TN, she has won numerous awards for her poetry.

Winifred Farrar, Meridian, MS, was featured in *Grandmother Earth VIII.* She is Poet Laureate of Mississippi.

Betty Gifford, 78 years old, almost native Memphian, transplanted to Denver, widow, 7 children, 16 grandchildren, almost 7 great-grandchildren, free-lance published writer for last 10 years. She has over 30 articles published in small religious magazines.

Dena R. Gorrell, Edmond, Oklahoma is a widely published writer who often wins national awards. She has been writing poetry since age nine. An avid poetry contestant, she always keeps something in the mail. She has published four books of poetry including *Truths, Tenderness and Trifles* and *Sunshine and Shadow.* She is often called upon to judge poetry contests at the local, state, and national levels. She wins about 100 awards per year.

Malu Graham, Memphis, TN, won the Hackney Award for fiction (Birmingham Southern College). She has poems and short stories published in St. Petersburg Times, Emerald Coast Review, Octoberfest Mag, Broomstick. She won prizes in fiction from Florida Writers' Competition.

Stucki Gudmundson, Bountiful, Utah**,** is a published author, former Speech-language Pathologist, wife of Dr. Ariel George Gudmundson, mother of six children, grandmother of 26 grandchildren, and great grandmother of three great-grandchildren. Besides having numerous poems published, she has won national and state poetry awards. Her latest book publication is *Wishing You Christmas Joy,* which came out in 2002.

Rita Goodgame has 13 grandchildren and 2 great-grand children. She has received honorable mentions and/or awards from: NLAPW (Arkansas Pioneer Branch), *ByLine Magazine, Fordham University College @ 60 Anthology*, Arkansas Writers' Conference.

Nancy Roberts Hammer, Birmingham, AL 35216, is a 71-year old grandmother of 15 with six children. She has been winning awards since she started writing 12 years ago. She works part-time as a receptionist and is a member of the Third Order of St. Francis. "My life is full, blessed and interesting."

Dorothy Hatfield, Beebe, AR is a secretary for a literacy cooperative. Besides writing, her interests are theater, music, music theater and theater music.

Betty Heidelberger, Lexa, AR, has been published in several literary magazines and has won numerous awards. She is one of the organizers of the AR Poetry Day activities. She is president of the East Central Branch of Poets Roundtable of AR. She got the Merit Award in 1998 from the Poets' Roundtable of AR.

Leona Mason Heitsch, Bourbon, MO, is a Michigan born farmer's daughter, who after years of raising children and teaching, is involved full time in farming, poetry and peace advocacy.

Rebecca Davis Henderson, Madison, AL, is a native of Cullman, AL and has been published *in Grandmother Earth, Alalitcom,* and *Ordinary and Sacred as Blood: Alabama Women Speak.* She also had a poem selected for Huntville, AL, festival 2002. Her family photographs grace Grandmother Earth's covers in 2000 and 2001.

Nina Salley Hepburn, Germantown, TN, worked for years in radio and TV—writing commercials and news, as well as announcing-- after moving to Memphis from Sarasota, Florida. Worked at

WHER, the all-girl station as announcer and copywriter. She is working on her second novel, also short stories as well as poetry. Her agent is trying to place her first mystery/suspense--*The Killing Farm*, the story of a female serial killer set in East Tennessee in the early 20th Century. She is a retired real estate broker.

Verna Lee Hinegardner, Hot Springs, Poet Laureate of Arkansas, is past president of the AR Pioneer Branch of NLAPW; Past President of PRA; President of Roundtable Poets of Hot Springs; served 12 years on the board of NFSPS and chaired two of their national conventions; member of Poets' Study Club, Poetry Society of America, International Poetry Society, and is listed in The International Directory of Distinguished Leadership. Hinegardner was inducted into the AR Writers' Hall of Fame in 1991; won their Sybil Nash Abrams Award in 1973, 1979 and 1991; and received the AR Award of Merit in 1976 and 1983; and is the author of eleven books of poetry.

Cornelius Hogenbirk, Waretown, NJ, is a retired sales engineer. His hobbies are photography, gardening, and writing. His writing and photography have been in every issue of *Grandmother Earth.*

Elaine R. Howard, Norcross, GA, is author of Here and Now… and Beyond. She is a metaphysical playwright, inspirational poet. Her website is authorsden.com/elainehoward.

Elizabeth Howard, Crossville, TN, is the author of *Anemones,* Grandmother Earth, 1998 which contains poetry that had been previously published in journals and anthologies. She is a frequent award-winner.

Florence Hustedt, Clarks Summit, PA, Has had a "God-guided career." She has traveled cross country eight times and has lived joyously in NJ, PA, AR, Montana, and SC.

Ellen E. Hyatt, Summerville, SC, is on the faculty of Charleston Southern U, a member of the Poetry Society of SC and a Fellow of the Western Pennsylvania Writing Project. She has won awards and her works appear in a variety of publications including an essay in *Chicken Soup for the Sports Fan's Soul.*

Judith Bader Jones, has a line of cards using her photographs of flowers. Though from Fairway, Kansas, she has ties to TN which include a grandmother named Tennessee.

Jeanne S. Kelly, Madison, MS, is an English instructor at Holmes Community college in Ridgeland. A past president of the MS Poetry Society, she is currently recording secretary and Poet of the Year committee chairman. Married to Phillip L. Kelly, they have two grown sons and a beautiful granddaughter.

Anne-Marie Legan, Herrin, IL, received from Cader Publishing, Ltd. the 1998 International Poet Of The Year Chapbook Competition, $5,000 grand prize and publication of *My Soul's On A Journey.* In the last four years, since she first started writing she's won over a hundred awards, winning the "Distinguished Poet's Award," Sparrowgrass, Editor's Choice Awards, (different magazines) and the President's Award in 1996, 97, 98, 99, 2000 and 2001. Active in Southern IL Writer's Guild, she has published widely. In December of 2001 her mystery novel, *Tattoo of a Wolf Spider*, a twisting tale of murder, was published by Xlibria.

Angela Logsdon, Memphis, TN is a social worker and member of PST.

Tom McDaniel, professionally know as Thomas W. McDaniel, is a well-known attorney in Memphis, TN. He has been President, and is Poet Laureate Emeritus, Life Member and Honorary member of the PST.

Martha McNatt, Humboldt, TN, is a former teacher, and director of the Child Nutrition Program for Madison County Schools. She is the author of *Feeding the Flock,* a cookbook for church kitchens, published by Bethany House, and *A Heritage Revisited,* a commissioned work by First Christian Church, Jackson, TN. Her work has appeared in each of the Grandmother Earth anthologies, in *Grandmother Earth's Healthy and Wise Cookbook,* and in Life Press's *Our Golden Thread.*

Kolette Montague is from Centerville, UT.

Christine Moyer is a photogopher-poet from Lakewood, CO.

Rosalyn Ostler, is a co-author of *By The Throat* and helped produce *Nine One One*, an anthology. Other award-winning poems have been published nationally.

Laura Pheonix, Rochester, MN, is noted for her letters to the editor, newsletters, and has been a journaler, story teller and poet for 30 years. She has two daughters and six grandchildren.

Cherry Pryon is a copy editor and newspaper writer from Clinton, Kentucky, active in the First Methodist UMC. She also writes for *Hometown Magazine* in South Fulton.

Diana K. Rubin, Piscataway, NJ, is the author of several books of poetry, two collections of short stories and a cookbook. Her honors include nominations for Pushcart Prize and Pulitzer Prize in Poetry. She received a Poet of the Year Award in 1999 from Sparrowgrass Poetry Forum. Her new books are *BREATH OF THE SPIRITS* (stories, 1999, Bristol Banner Books) and *A GATHERED MEADOW* (Prospect Press, 2000).

LaVonne Schoneman, Seattle, WA is a former actress. Her husband, children and eight grandchildren also reside in WA. She is author of the popular How to Cope series on coping with post-polio, she also writes (and judges) fiction and poetry.

N. Colwell Snell, Born and raised in Cowley, Wyoming. Moved to Utah in 1967 and has lived there since. Graduated from the University of Utah with BA in English and taught for a short period in Utah high schools prior to establishing his own financial services firm in 1977. Serves on the board of the Utah State Poetry Society. His poetry has won awards locally and nationally and has been published in several anthologies, including Poetry Panorama, Encore, Bay Area Poets Coalition, California Quarterly and Anthology magazine. He is co-author of By the Throat, Selected Poems. Hobbies include basketball, golf, and fishing. He and his wife, Barbara, have two sons.

Marilyn Stacy, a Dallas psychotherapist, writes poetry, fiction and nonfiction. Her poems can be found in anthologies, journals and her own books, *Along the Path* and *Dreams.*

Ruth L. Stewart, Mechanicsville, VA, is a new member of Life Press and associate member of PST. A former Language Arts teacher and Literary Media Specialist from Richmond Public Schools, she has had poems published in several magazines including *Shining Star, Mature Living, Purpose Magazine* and *Lutheran Digest.*

Russell Strauss, Memphis, TN, has won numerous awards in the NFSPS contests. His "Unknown Warriors" won a grand prize in the PA contest and the "Trail of Tears" won a first plass in PA.

Walt Stromer, Mt.Vernon, IA, is retired from teaching communication courses and now doing some free lance writing, Born in Nebraska, he spent some time in the Army, went to college in Nebraska then U. of Denver.

Brett Taylor, Knoxville, TN, is originally from Wartsburg, TN. He has published in *South by SouthEast, Raw Nervz Haiku, Haiku Headlines, Persimmon, Modern Haiku, Cicada,* and *Cotyledon.*

Vincent J. Tomeo, Flushing, NY, won honorable mention in the Rainer Maria Rilke International Poetry Competition, 1999. He has had 71 poems published in anthologies, newspapers, magazines and on the tape, "The Sound of Poetry."

Dr. Malra Treece is Professor Emeritus, College of Business and Economics, University of Memphis. She is author of thirteen college textbooks and has just published the seventh edition of *Successful Communication in Business and the Profession.*

Ruth Whittenburg is from Bella Vista, AR.

Alice Heard Williams, Lynchburg, VA is a poet and art historian with three books of poetry published including "Hey, Madame Matisse!" a book of poems about paintings which received a national award. Her novel, *Seeking the High Yellow Note, Vincent Van Gogh in Provence* was published in 2002.

STUDENT CONTRIBUTORS

Patrick Banks, Christina Brooks and Tommie Franklin, Memphis, TN, are 11th grade art students of Frances Cowden at Northside High School.

Bethany Byrd, Ticara Gaillard, Sarah Nolen, Memphis, TN were 12th grade students of Ms. Enek at Overton High when they did these Eye-poems.

Aishah LeAnadra El-Akkan, Daytona Beach, FL is 14. She is a member of FSPA, and Life Poets Society. She aspires to be a photojournalist for *National Geographic.*

Laurie Skelton, grade 11, attends Jefferson County International Baccalaurate High School, Birmingham, AL.

Melissa Taylor, Little Rock, AR, is sixteen years old and enjoys soccer and is a goal keeper. She has won awards in Byline Magazine and at the Arkansas Writers' Conference. She is in Grade 11 at Pulaski Academy.

Christopher and Courtney Watts, attend Ilchester Elementary in Ellicott City, MD. Christopher's third grade teacher was Mrs. Beamer, and Coutney's fifth grade teacher was Ms. Schneider.

Katie Williams wrote her poem while in the seventh grade at Sloan–Hendrix Elementary, Imboden, AR.

FLORIDA CONTRIBUTORS

Barbara Abbott, Pencolo Beach, FL, is a retired art and English teacher from Shelby County, TN. A life member of PST, she edited *Grandmother Earth's Healthy and Wise Cook Book.*

Laurie Boulton, Melbourne, FL, [pen name Lauri Silver] BA,

M.Ed.; retired. Published in journals and specialized magazines, *Kicker, Grapevine*; newspapers, *Florida Today*. Won several non-fiction short story/essay awards and numerous poetry awards in many states. Her specialty area is photography to illustrate poems for and about veterans.

Bill Caudle, Summertown, TN is a Florida Native. He is an attorney [still licensed in Florida] and published author: he has published legal treatises and historical fiction, notably *The Canal* in 1999 and a vignette recently published in *The Irriantum*, a quarterly magazine. Bill and his wife Cheri are writing a musical play entitled *Pennington's Dream*, about Lawrence County's own "Aerial Bird" inventor, James Jackson Pennington, which will be produced in 2003, the centennial year of the Wright Brothers' flight at Kitty Hawk, North Carolina.

Audrey Cooke, Dayton, FL, is a native New Yorker. Her widely published poems have captured over 60 awards, and her short story, "When Does the Tide Change" appeared in *Vision Magazine.*

Anna DeMay, Orange Park, FL, has published in numerous journals, including *Spindrift, State Street Review,* and *West Wind Review.*

Erwin Doege, Panama City Beach, FL, sketches came from his sketch book while living in Miami in the 60's. He began writing poetry in 1997 after losing his vision. His art had been represented in many cities. He now paints with words.

Miriam Doege, Panama City Beach, FL, has been active in poetry circles for several years. Formally from AR where she was a member of Poets No. West and PRA. She is an award-wining, published poet. She and her husband Erwin are members of the Emerald Coast Poets in Panama City and the FSPA

Susan Leeds, Delay Beach, FL, is an award-winning poet. Publications include: *Mid-West Poetry Review, Pegasus, The Pen Women Magazine, Lucidity,* and *Wyoming, The Hub of the Wheel....* She is a member of NLAPW, the FLSA.

C. E. Larsen, St. Petersburg, FL has also lived in Miami. Writing is a passion which has been pursued for more than 50 years and is more important to him than ever before.

Pearl S. Lupin, Ft. Lauderdale, FL, is a retired educator with work published in magazines and newspapers in the US and foreign countries. Her song lyrics have been performed in state and international conventions. .

Frances Muir, South Florida, has been a teacher, electronics technologist and technical writer.

June Owens, Zephyrhills, Florida, is 75 years old and has published many poems and won many prizes. Her first book of poetry, *Tree Line,* published by Prospect Press won the Sparrowgrass Poet of the Year.

Meg Roman, Zephyrhills, FL is an elementary art teacher, an artist, and a member of New River Poets Group in Wesley Chapel. She is a member of the FLSA. and the NFSPS.

Bonnie L. Warner, Port Orange, FL, is editor of FLSA's Of Poets and Poetry, editor of *Wildfire!* Florida, 1998. Credits include: *Grandmother Earth, Poets' Forum Magazine, Blue Mountain Arts, Penumbra, Harp-Strings Poetry Journal,* anthologies and local newspapers.

GRANDMOTHER EARTH PUBLICATIONS

Prices quoted apply only if ordered from Grandmother Earth

Abbott, Barbara, *GRANDMOTHER EARTH'S HEALTHY AND WISE COOKBOOK,* 1-884289-13-4 Healthy and easy cooking, but not diet. First layer of fat skimmed from Southern cooking. Optabind binding; $11.

Benedict, Burnette Bolin, *KINSHIP,* 1-884289-08--Lyrical poetry by Knoxville poet. Chapbook, 1995, $6.

Cowden, Frances Brinkley, *VIEW FROM A MISSISSIPPI RIVER COTTON SACK,* 1-884289-03-7. This collection of poetry and short prose emphasizes family values and farm life in Mississippi County, Arkansas and life in Memphis, Tennessee. Cloth, gold imprint, 1993, $15.

TO LOVE A WHALE; 1-884289-06-1. Learn about endangered animals from children and educators. Children's drawings, poetry and prose, PB (Perfect bound) 1995, $8.

BUTTERFLIES AND UNICORNS, ED 4, 1-884289-04-5 (Cowden and Hatchett) Poetry for the young and young-at-heart with notes on teaching creative writing. PB, 1994, $8.

Daniel, Jack, *SOUTHERN RAILWAY- FROM STEVENSON TO MEMPHIS*—1-884289-17-7. 1/2x 11with 400+ photographs, 360 pages, 1996. Daniel is an Alabama native who now lives in Cordova, TN. Documents and other papers with heavy emphasis upon history of Southern Railway and its workers. PB, $29.
MY RECOLLECTIONS OF CHEROKEE, ALABAMA, 1-884289-25, 8 1/2x11. 300+ photographs of author's family history and life in early Cherokee, 232 pages, PB, 1998, $22.
THOROUGHBREDS OF RAILROADING: YESTERDAY AND TODAY, ISBN 1-884289-26-6 1999, 312 pages, 8 1/2x 11, pictorial history of several railroads. PB, $29.

Hatchett, Eve Braden, *TAKE TIME TO LAUGH*: It's the Music of the Soul. 1- 884289-00-2. Humorous poetry taking off on Eden theme. Chapbook, very limited edition, 1993, $9.

Howard, Elizabeth, *ANEMONES*, 1-884289-27-4, Prize-winning poetry, all previously published, East Tennessee (Crossville) poet, introduction by Connie Green, creative writing instructor, U.T. 1998, $9.

Schirz, Shirley Rounds, *ASHES TO OAK*, 1-884289-07-X Poetry of the lakes region by widely-published Wisconsin author. Grandmother Earth chapbook winner, 1995, $6.

GRANDMOTHER EARTH SERIES: $8 each (multiple copies $7 each, Volume II is $5) Order by Volume number.
GRANDMOTHER EARTH II and III feature Tennessee writers. Volume IV features Arkansas Writers. Volume VII features Alabama writers. Volume VIII features Mississippi.

LIFE PRESS PUBLICATIONS

Boren, Blanche S., *THORNS TO VELVET. Devotionals from a Lifetime of Christian Experience*. 1-884289- 231, Blanche S. Boren, Kivar 7, gold imprint, cloth, $18.

Cowden, Frances Brinkley, *OUR GOLDEN THREAD*: *Dealing with Grief,* 1-884289-10-x, Ed. Personal testimonies and poetry of 40 contributors from clergy and lay writers who deal with different kinds of grief using personal experiences in their faith journeys. Kivar 7 cloth, gold imprint, 1996, $15.

ANGELS MESSENGERS OF LOVE AND GRACE, 1-884289-18-5. True stories of angel experiences by contributors from all walks of life. 96 pages, perfect bound, 1999, $10.

TOWARD IMAGERY AND FORM: A WRITER'S NOTE-BOOK, 1-8884289-29-0. Loose leaf or coil notebook which contains lessons on strengthening writing skills though poetry and prose lessons. Editing, imagery and poetry forms are stressed. Many forms used are explained. Prize-winning examples by contemporary poets. Lessons were from the first five years of Life Press Writers' Association.

Crow, Geraldine Ketchum, BLOOM WHERE YOU ARE TRANSPLANTED, 1-884289-12-6. A resident of Little Rock, Arkansas, Crow grew up in Hot Springs and tells of life in Perry County where she and her husband farmed for several years. Humorous, inspirational approach about moving from the city to the country. PB, 1996, $10.

Davis, Elaine Nunnally, *MOTHERS OF JESUS: FROM MATTHEW'S GENEALOGY,* 1-884289-05-3. Biography of five women mentioned in Matthew. 344 pp. PB, 1994, $11.

EVES FRUIT, 1-884289-11-8, Defense of Eve and implications for the modern woman. PB, 1995, $10.

The sixth annual **Life Press Christian Writers Conference (with national contest)** will be held in August, 2003 in Memphis, TN. Write P. O. Box 241986, Memphis, TN 38124 for more information after March, 2003, or download from www.grandmotherearth.com.

PATRONS

Thanks to Nancy Johnson
at Grahamwood Elementary for being an inspiration.
John, Debbie and Stephanie McVean.

Antiques Plus
Auction and Antique Mall—870-739-5856
Exit 14, I-55, Marion, AR

Marina Brinkley—901- 619-4023
Prudential Collins/Maury, Inc., Realtors
I can help sell your old house and buy your dream home.

Memphis Woman's Yellow Pages
BUSINESS LISTINGS
www.memphiswyp.com

A View From the South
By Lorraine A. Smith
A collection of personal anecdotes taken from the humorous, nostalgic and touching columns originally published in the *Collierville Herald*. Hard cover with gold imprint. Order from the author at 464 Burley Rd., Collierville, TN 38017. $20 plus $1.50 postage.

Thomas W. McDaniel
Attorney at Law
46 N. Third, Suite 730
Memphis, Tennessee 38103
Phone: (901) 525-8612
Fax: (901) 527-0450

IN MEMORIAM

Glenna Jane Sisk Winchester
June 19, 1940—February 8, 2002
Daughter of Virgil and Winnie Sisk
Niece of Coy Dean Cowden

Harold Winston Perry
July 28, 1926—April 8, 2002
Faithful Leader and Teacher at
Colonial Park United Methodist Church
Husband of Jackie Perry

Rosemary Carswell Stephens
December 4, 1924—July 17, 2002
Patron of and contributor to the first eight issues of
Grandmother Earth
Wife of Harold Stephens

John Fredrick Werne
June 27, 1920—September 28, 2002
Faithful Leader and Servant at
Colonial Park United Methodist Church
Husband of Catherine Werne

Rev. Thomas Fredrick Mooring
September 28, 1924—October 25, 2002
Faithful Teacher and Servant
Husband of Grace Bullard Mooring
Uncle of Frances Brinkley Cowden

Index

Abbott, cover, 63

Arceneaux, 33, 43

Banks, 62

Boulton, 76, 77, 78

Brown, 32

Byrd, 65

Cannizzo, 16, 30

Chandler, 49

Cooke, 88

Cowden, 46

Darby, 24

Dorris, 45

Doege, M., 80

Farrar, 36

Gaillard, 64

Goodgame, 14

Graham, 3

Hammer, 39

Heidelberger, 37

Henderson, 38, 48

Hinegardner, 27

Howard, Elizabeth, 19

Allen, 29

Adams, 10, 14

Black, 8

Brooks, 60

Bruce, 40

Camp, 16

Caudle, 84

Clemmons, 2, 6

Copening, 33

Crawford, 44

DeMay, 71

Doege, E., 68, 82

El-Akkari, 64, 83

Franklin, 63

Gifford, 25

Gorrell, 36

Gudmundson, 43

Hatfield, 92

Heitsch, 12

Hepburn, 17

Hogenbirk, *viii*, 56, 95

Howard, Elaine, 28

Hustedt, 13

Hyatt, 18

Jones, 47

Kelly, 25

Larsen, 74

Leeds, 79, 80

Legan, 22

Logsdon, 17

Lupin, 71

McDaniel, 34

McNatt, 35

Montague, 38

Moyer, 10, 20

Muir, 72, 73

Nolen, 67

Ostler, 37

Owens, 75

Pheonix, 48

Pyron, 58

Rice, 1

Rubin, 30

Roman, 78

Schoneman, 7

Skelton, 62

Smith, 14

Snell, 4, 5

Stacy. 42

Stewart, 21

Strauss, 11, 15, 23

Stromer, 7

Taylor, B., 18, 26

Taylor, M., 61

Tomeo, 24, 42

Treece, 53

Warner, *ii, viii*, 69, 87

Watts, Chris, 63

Watts, Courtney, 66

Whittenberg, 9

Williams, A., 31, 41

Williams, K., 65